Dark Goddess
Magick

Dark Goddess Magick

RITUALS AND SPELLS FOR RECLAIMING YOUR FEMININE FIRE

C. ARA CAMPBELL

FAIR WINDS

© 2021 Quarto Publishing Group USA Inc.
Text © 2021 C. Ara Campbell
Illustrations © 2021 Mary Ancilla Martinez

First Published in 2021 by Fair Winds Press, an imprint of The Quarto Group,
100 Cummings Center, Suite 265-D, Beverly, MA 01915, USA.
T (978) 282-9590 F (978) 283-2742 QuartoKnows.com

Fair Winds Press titles are also available at discount for retail, wholesale, promotional, and bulk purchase. For details, contact the Special Sales Manager by email at specialsales@quarto.com or by mail at The Quarto Group, Attn: Special Sales Manager, 100 Cummings Center, Suite 265-D, Beverly, MA 01915, USA.

25 24 23 22   3 4 5

ISBN: 978-0-7603-7095-7

Digital edition published in 2021
eISBN: 978-0-7603-7096-4

Library of Congress Cataloging-in-Publication Data available.

Design and layout: Laura Shaw Design, Inc.
Illustrations: Mary Ancilla Martinez, @maryancilla.art, www.maryancilla.com

Printed in USA

To my family,
my dog Sonny, and
my global circle.
Thank you for the love
and support.

Contents

Introduction

Everything that we've been taught about our dark side has been a lie.

We've heard it all before: "Smile through the pain." "Swallow your anger." "Don't make waves." "Keep your voice down." These are the mantras we have been brainwashed with, that have shaped our beliefs and fed our fears our entire lives—all the while silencing our truth. We have been told that anything that isn't positive or pleasant is wrong. And for what? To make us manageable, digestible, and easy to deal with.

But who wants to be easy to deal with, anyway?

For centuries, we lived in a society that was afraid of our truth. Any differentiation from the status quo was seen as anarchy, and we were dealt with accordingly. We were burned as witches, persecuted, ostracized, and shunned. We held our breath waiting for the ax to fall. We learned early that expressing our truth would be bad and we sacrificed our medicine. The knowledge and practices of the dark goddesses were kept from our view and labeled as evil. "Demon," they whispered. "Harlot." "Witch."

These lies were meant to destroy her, but in the darkness her power grew. Now a new dawn is rising—one that will see us embrace our medicine and awaken.

Deep transformation occurs when we connect to the ancient wisdom of the dark goddesses. Through her practices and rituals, we can reshape our world. By embracing our darkness and dancing with our shadows, we embrace the truth of all that we are. The wisdom in these myths aids us in finding our truth.

In this book, I will show you how to connect with the magick of the dark goddesses and how to access her for transformation in your life. Through her rituals, visualizations, and practices, we can enable healing, release, and growth. By reclaiming the rites that have been shunned in the past and buried for their "darkness," we reclaim a hidden part of our power.

I awakened to my destined path with the creation of The Goddess Circle after a dark night of the soul. A writer and teacher at heart, I had silenced my dream to help others. Instead, I followed the path that society taught me I should want: my own office, my name on the door, and a steady income following someone else's dream. I had made it, but I felt emptier than ever. I was surrounded by people who only stood beside me when they needed something from me. I was lost. I was disillusioned with the structure I had been taught that I needed to aspire to, and my soul was crying to break free.

I had moved away from my origins as a child enamored with the myths of the goddess, the wisdom that lay in the unseen world, and the medicine of the earth. I ignored my own creative self, and I was drowning in a sea of conformity as a result. It was the winter of 2014 when the goddess Inanna found me in the darkness. After a deep dive into the underworld with the goddess, I was reborn. I remembered the ancient knowledge of the priestess etched upon my bones and the medicine I was here to share with the world. I knew that I needed to release what no longer served my path. Through the portal of the dark goddess and her magick, this priestess had at long last come home to her truth.

Now, in every aspect of my work, I strive to unlock this portal of rebirth for others. Since awakening to my own path in 2014, I have connected with women around the world. I have led online global circles, created and facilitated courses, and conceived goddess-centered practices as a powerful tool of transformation. We unearth unparalleled wisdom when working with her mystery. Within the arms of the goddess, all things are transformed. Much like the goddess Aradia, my chosen namesake, I am here to share with the world the mysteries of the old ways written on my soul.

This book explores the myths of the darker goddesses and applies their wisdom to practices and rituals dedicated to dropping us deeper into our own truth. You will hear the stories of the goddesses and learn how you can apply their insight to your life to create great change. This book does not attempt to prove these beings have ever lived; instead, we will tap into their powerful archetypal energy for our own expansion.

As we move deeper into *her* great mystery, our truth is revealed. As we embrace our truth, our medicine is born. We have now entered a great age of expansion that is shaking the foundations of the earth upon which we stand. Transformation is upon us, as is a global dark night of the soul as we face the dawning of a new era. The dark goddess walks this path alongside us, and she has a message: The time has come to rise.

Deep bow to your unfolding path,
C. ARA CAMPBELL

How to Use This Book

WORKING WITH THE ENERGY OF THE DARK GODDESSES

When we connect with the stories of the goddesses, we connect with their energy and wisdom. We can use the goddess myths to dive deeper into transformation, knowledge, and growth, though that doesn't mean that the goddesses existed. Some had roots in real people, such as Aradia as *La Bella Pellegrina*, but most exist in legend.

Dark Goddesses are not evil. They deal with shadows, fear, abandonment, healing, and the unseen. They are the ones in the trenches with us when things get dirty, walking with us during dark nights of the soul.

When we work with these goddesses, we connect with energy that exists within the feminine and masculine forces of the universe. All aspects apply to any being, no matter how they self identify. As we connect deeper with our own unfolding and ever-evolving truth, we expand the old definitions of these archetypes, far beyond the limitations of the oppressive structures of the past. We can be warrior, nurturer, and wise sage in the same breath. There are no constraints on our expression.

The goddess visualizations in this book are a way to connect with the energy of each goddess for empowerment and expansion. The practices and rituals are a tangible way to channel this energy to manifest the desired change in our world. And the incantations and affirmations are powerful for directly connecting to the energy of the goddess.

MOON PHASES AND CALLING A CIRCLE

Some rituals in this book specify times for their use. These are guidelines; feel free to change them as inspired. As a general rule, banishing work is done as the moon is waning or during the dark of the moon. Drawing is done during the waxing moon or full moon.

Each practice can be done on its own or in a circle. Calling a circle before a ritual practice can be helpful to clearly define your intentions, provide protection, and strengthen your spell. Circles can also be called during special occasions, such as the new moon, the full moon, or during sacred festivals or celebrations, to connect with the powerful energy.

You can call a simple circle before your rite by envisioning a circle of light surrounding your work. Call each of the cardinal directions (north, east, south, and west) and elements (earth, air, fire, and water) to be present. Walk clockwise around your intended area, visualizing a circle on the ground, and say:

I call in the powers of our Mother Earth and her blessings from the North
May she aid in bringing my manifestation forth
I call in the powers from the East, the blessings of Sky and Air
Let my space be swept of all ill and left clear
I call in the powers from the South, the flame of sacred fire
Let this space be protected and a vessel for my desire
I call in the powers of Water and Wave, and her blessings from the West
Let this space be empowered and let this rite be blessed.

When you are finished, trace back the circle in the opposite direction. Thank each of the elements and cardinal points for their help, and release the energy.

OFFERINGS

I believe in thanking the powers that wish to co-create with us, so I leave a natural sacred offering outside after the rite or practice is complete. Some ideas for the natural item to leave are seeds for the birds, a crystal, herbs, or flowers.

When crafting your rites, keep salts, oils, herbs, and smoke away from children and pets, as you never know who will have an allergy. When using herbs, use ones that are more culinary based and avoid toxic ones. Herbs should be kept away from curious children and fur babies. When using salt outside, keep it away from any plants to avoid damaging them.

When looking for items from nature, gather ones that have fallen, such as branches, to cause as little harm to the tree as possible. When taking herbs or leaves from nature, only take a small amount, never all of the plant. Give reverence to the natural world that is providing, ask permission, and give thanks.

After you are done with your rite, do something to bring yourself back into the present moment, such as grounding, releasing energy back to the earth, yoga, or a walk to center your energy.

ITEMS LISTED IN THE SPELLS

Each practice in this book features suggested items that carry an intended energy for that rite. If you don't have the item on hand or you don't feel like using that specific item, feel into your intuition and what you are called to use. Rituals are unique to the person crafting them, so make them your own. Honor what you are called to use or what you have on hand. White or natural candles can be used in place of any colored candle. Salt can be used in place of protective herbs, and a small fireproof container is a perfect stand-in for a bonfire.

    If specific herbs are hard to find, you can find some in tea form. Mint, yarrow, chamomile, and nettle can usually be found in the tea aisle. Dried culinary herbs from the grocery can substitute for any fresh herb. Rosemary, thyme, basil, and sage are all readily available.

HEXES AND CURSES

Not everyone feels comfortable using hexes or curses, and that is okay. I believe hexes are self-defense when used in a protective manner toward someone who has intentionally tried to hurt you. If someone has the intention to force your will or cause you harm, you have the right to defend yourself. If you don't want to use a hex, you can do protective or shielding rituals instead.

SEEKING OUTSIDE HELP

If you need to, please take the proper precautions and contact the correct channels, such as police or lawyers for protection, a medical professional for illness, or a counselor for emotional healing. The rituals in this book are to be used in tandem with conventional healing methods and are not a substitute for proper medical treatment. Do not ingest any unknown herbs or crystals. Take care with candles; use them only in ventilated areas and in places clear of debris.

INTENT

Make your intentions and desires clear. If you don't, unexpected occurrences can happen. For example, you might put a protection spell on your home because you fear losing it, but someone could still try to buy it and lease it back to you. So your home would be safe, but technically no longer yours. Be specific in your wording and crystal-clear in your intent and what you want.

1

HECATE

GODDESS OF MAGICK

- - -

THE WITCH

MOON GODDESS

WITCH QUEEN

DARK SORCERESS

CRONE

CREATRIX OF SPELLS

GODDESS OF MAGICK

- - -

Hecate (or Hekate) is the Greek goddess connected with dark magick, the gift of prophecy, the underworld, and the energy of the moon. She is said to have three faces and is often represented as the crone aspect in a goddess triad with Persephone as maiden and Demeter as mother. She is a descendant of the Titan god Perses and nymph Asteria.

HECATE INVOCATION

"Oh Hecate, dark sorceress who stands at the crossroads of life and death, hear my call. When the path before me is shrouded, I seek your wise counsel. Guide me through the mysteries that lay in the unseen. Grant me your eyes, so that I may see beyond the shadows. Grant me your insight, so that I may connect to the knowledge of the universe. Grant me your courage, so that I may walk forward on the road meant for me. So it is."

HECATE'S PATH is that of the witch, and she imparts her great knowledge and protection to those who follow the old ways. She knows the mysteries locked inside of each herb, plant, and stone, and she shared those teachings with her witches. As she is connected so heavily to the natural world and the powers of the earth, some myths portray her as an agriculture goddess protecting fields and farmers from harm by day. By night, she leans toward the occult, cemeteries, and tombs, spending time connecting with spirits in the Underworld. In this way she is a multifaceted goddess who holds great power over the mysteries of the earth, underworld, sea, and heaven.

Crossroads are sacred to her, especially ones with three paths. Ancient Athenians often left tributes and offerings at crossroads in reverence to her. Hecate is connected with divination, as she can see into the dark unknown.

Hecate spends time in the underworld, where spirits follow her wherever she goes. Hounds are sacred to her, and dogs can see her when she visits the earthly realm. She has a black canine familiar who is said to have once been Queen Hecuba of Troy. When Hecuba attempted to take her own life after the fall of Troy, Hecate transformed her into a dog and kept her at her side as a companion.

Hecate is a goddess of many faces, but at her core she is deeply connected with the dark mysteries of the universe. Whenever we walk through times of uncertainty or darkness, Hecate is a powerful ally. The Lady at the Crossroads reminds us to pay attention and open our eyes so we can see all paths ahead. Hecate tells us we often need to step back and spend some time in solitude to come to the decision we need.

Hecate is connected with the old ways, and spending time studying the mysteries of the earth, the stars, and the spirits. She is also a creatrix of rituals and spellcraft, and is often the goddess chosen in times of need by those who practice her craft.

STANDING AT THE CROSSROADS

When we face times of great uncertainty in our lives, Hecate can be a powerful force to guide us.

Lie down in a safe, comfortable place and take a few deep, centering breaths. Close your eyes and relax your body.

Envision yourself standing in a vast, open space. Notice that you are in the middle of the crossroads, and standing in front of you is the goddess Hecate.

"You have come here seeking wisdom from the goddess Hecate for the path ahead. You desire guidance and illumination on the choices that you must now make. Come, my child, stand with me here at the crossroads and speak aloud what troubles thee."

Tell Hecate what choices, issues, or fears you are struggling with, and the goddess will present two paths from the crossroads.

"On each road is a choice, one that only you can make. Each of these paths will lead you in a different direction. Walk forward now and see where your path leads. Open yourself to the wisdom that is revealed to you."

Walk towards the road that calls to you. Notice there is a black dog standing on the path ahead. It holds a scroll in its mouth.

"This is my familiar, my shadow hound who travels between all known and unknown worlds. She sees all and knows all. She has brought for you an answer to your inquiry, a key to that which you seek. Take the scroll from her and take this message to heart."

Take the scroll and read the message, which gives you insight into your question. Take a moment to be present with what is revealed to you.

"Heed these words, and pay attention to the signs that reveal themselves to your heart. Trust your feet as you travel upon your road. Blessings to you on the path forward."

Bring attention back to your body, slowly open your eyes, and take a few deep breaths. As you step back into your day, take Hecate's guidance and messages with you.

Matters Associated with Hecate

* Making decisions
* Need for clarity or insight
* Witchcraft, spells, or rituals
* Cycles of life, death, and rebirth
* Hexes, banishing, and protection
* Getting our needs met
* Releasing or clearing
* Divination and visions
* Honoring the moon
* Change or transformation
* Traversing the dark night of the soul
* Honoring ancestors and the deceased
* Connection with spirits

Hecate Affirmation

"I make decisions that are in alignment with my highest good and deepest truth. I honor my own path forward. I make choices that honor my needs and desires. I am a channel for divine wisdom and magick. I see the truth in all situations. I have the power to manifest anything in my life. I move forward confidently on my own path."

Hecate Associations

CRYSTALS	Moonstone, black tourmaline, quartz, pearl, labradorite, smoky quartz
COLORS	Black, silver, gray
PLANTS & OILS	Cypress, lavender, cardamom, myrrh, sage, anise, belladonna (poisonous), cyclamen, dandelion, garlic, date, hemlock (poisonous), mint, oak, willow, mandrake (poisonous), wolfsbane (poisonous)
ARCHETYPES	The Witch. Moon Goddess. Witch Queen. Dark Sorceress. Crone. Creatrix of Spells. Goddess of Magick.
SYMBOLS	The crossroads, dogs, spirits, ghosts, graves, two torches, X, the underworld

DARK MOON CLARITY

The dark moon is a powerful time for prophecy and for gaining deeper insight into the unseen world. During this time of darkness, we can dive deeper into the shadows. Hecate is the perfect goddess to guide us, with her gifts of insight into the unseen and her connection to the underworld.

SUPPLIES
Pen and paper; Candle

During the dark moon phase, light a candle and write down what you require clarity on. This can be a situation, a relationship, or anything that requires aid. Stare into the flame and say:

"Dark moon, dark moon
Tell me what you see.
Guide me deeper
With clarity."

Allow yourself to focus on the flame and let your mind wander. Notice where your mind goes. When you are finished, blow out the candle and go to sleep. Pay attention to any messages you receive in your dreams or in the days to come.

BREAKING A HEX

At times, we may feel like things are not going our way. We may even feel like someone has put a curse on us, or that we are caught in an endless loop of bad luck. It can be frustrating, but the goddess Hecate is here to help. As she protects and aids her followers, she can help us break negative energy directed towards us. This spell can be done during the waning moon, during the dark moon, or at sunset.

SUPPLIES
2 small, dry sticks; Pen
Rosemary, sprig or dried; Sage, leaf or dried;
Black candle

Gather the items. Write the name of the person you think has caused you harm on each of the sticks. If you don't know, you could write "foe of mine" or "the one who wishes me harm." Place the two sticks on the ground in an X formation with the candle in the middle. Sprinkle the herbs on the X. Light the candle and say:

"Goddess Hecate, hear my call.
Aid me from those who would watch me fall.
Guard me against negativity
And banish all evil from me.
To those that wish me harm or ill,
The goddess Hecate now brings your fill.
What you send forth comes back on thee.
As I will it, so shall it be."

Pick up one of the sticks, hold it in both of your hands, and say:

"I now break any hexes or curses that be
Pointed in any way, shape, or form toward me."

Break one stick in half, envisioning the bad luck and negativity breaking with it. Pick up the second stick and say:

"All that was ill, all that was vile
Is shattered now and sent to exile.
No more evil is sent toward me,
All negativity is lifted from me."

Break the second stick, envisioning the negative intentions being broken and severed. Take the broken sticks and herbs to a place they can be buried or burned. As you dispose of them, say:

"Thank you, Hecate, for hearing my plea
All hexes now away from me flee. So it is."

HECATE SMUDGE RECIPE

Smudging can be done before or after rituals, anytime we wish to clear the air, or when the energy in our environment has grown stagnant. These herbs can also be left as an offering.

SUPPLIES
1 tablespoon (1 g) dried cypress; ½ teaspoon (1 g) dried lavender;
4 tablespoons (2 g) crushed dried sage leaves

Combine the herbs and store in a tightly sealed jar until ready to use.

Burn in fireproof container. Use it in a well-ventilated area, and keep it away from anything that could suffer from smoke damage. Never leave it unattended, and keep it away from pets and children.

WITCH BOTTLE OF PROTECTION

Witch bottles are powerful protective folk talismans often buried near the home to ward off negativity, hexes, and ill will. They are filled with sharp objects said to stop evil from entering the home and vinegar or urine to drown the evil. Hair or nail clippings from members of the household are added to fortify who receives the protection. As animals are sacred to Hecate, add a little hair from your pets to the jar! Craft this Witch Bottle of Protection during the waning moon to protect your home and banish negativity.

SUPPLIES

Black candle; Sealable jar or bottle with a stopper; Sharp items (pins, nails, thorns, broken glass); Sea salt; Bay leaf; Rosemary; Cloves; Burdock root; Hair from each person/pet living in the hom; Vinegar; Shovel or trowel; Offering

Gather all the items and bring them to your chosen sacred space. Light the black candle and hold your hands over the items:

> *"I dedicate this witch bottle to the protection of my household.*
> *May all negativity be repelled from here tenfold.*
> *As I will it, so it is."*

Fill the bottle with the sharp items, salt, herbs, and hair, holding the intention of protection as you do. Envision negative forces being repelled from your home and yard. When all the items are in, add the vinegar to the bottle and say:

> *"Mighty Hecate, guard us well.*
> *Protect those within these walls that dwell.*
> *Banish all evil, ill, and harm.*
> *Give power to this witch's charm.*
> *Watch over your children, goddess Hecate.*
> *As I will it, so shall it be."*

Seal the jar lid with the wax from the black candle. Bury the jar in an undisturbed place near the home, such as under steps, at the edge of your property, or under a nearby tree or bush. When you are finished with the ritual, thank the goddess Hecate for hearing your petition.

2

KALI

WARRIORESS AND GREAT DESTROYER

WARRIORESS

DARK MOTHER

DESTROYER

THE WILD FEMININE

THE BLACK GODDESS

Kali is a powerful Hindu goddess of death, transformation, creation, rebirth, and time. She is often called Kali Ma, the divine mother, or dark mother. In her destroyer aspect, she is shown as a fierce, feral goddess with four arms, blue or dark skin, severed arms around her waist, and a necklace of skulls. She is often depicted with her tongue pointed down and out of her open mouth.

KALI INVOCATION

"Fierce one. Warrioress. Destroyer of obstacles. Embodiment of the fierce feminine. Destroy the forces that push against me. Release all that no longer serves my highest good. As I take up your sword, I fight my battles with courage and move my plans forward. I honor what is in my highest good and release all that is no longer needed. I am Kali, as Kali is me."

KALI is the creatrix of the universe, and she holds the power of time, rebirth, chaos, and destruction. She is a force to call upon to clear away what is no longer needed and to tap into a powerful energy of transformation. She rules the untamed, unbridled aspect of feminine strength and fury. She is the goddess to connect with when petitioning for powerful transformation, clearing, and complete change. She has many faces, though many paint her solely as a battle-frenzied demon and bloodthirsty monster. She is a warrior, the embodiment of the wild, ferocious, feminine fire that burns within us all.

Kali has many legends surrounding her origin. In many of her myths, the gods created her to slay demons no other could vanquish. She became the great devourer, taking all these demons into herself in order to end their destruction. In the aftermath, she became bloodthirsty and destroyed all she could see until she was stopped by the god Shiva, her husband.

Kali is seen as a protectress and defender of her people, as well as the creative force of the universe. Kali does what needs to be done, no matter how terrible, raising her sword in defense and protection. As a force of transformation, truth, and revolution, Kali calls to us to tear away what is no longer needed in our lives, burning away the old and unneeded so rebirth can occur. She bids us to dance with our fears so they can no longer hold us prisoner. She strips away the veil from every aspect of our lives and shows us everything in raw truth, even when it is hard to see.

The goddess Kali calls to us to take back our power—to reclaim our voices, our sexuality, and our intense emotions. Kali teaches us there is nothing wrong when it comes to the fierce aspects of the feminine, and there is nothing for us to hide. She teaches us that in these shadows, there is much for us to see and many lessons to learn. She tells us that by looking at what is keeping us stuck, we start the cycle of rebirth and transforming it into what we want. When we move past the blocks and clear them, what we are left with is potent soil in which to plant the seeds of our desires. Kali asks that we dance in her fire and burn away all that no longer serves us.

DEMON BANISHING WITH THE SWORD OF KALI

Kali is a goddess of protection and destruction known for freeing the land from the grip of voracious demons that held sway. She can help us to free ourselves from the demons and issues that bind us in our own lives.

Lie down in a safe, comfortable place and take a few deep, centering breaths. Close your eyes and relax your body.

You find yourself in a dark landscape, clouds forming in the sky overhead. In front of you stands Kali, holding a sword to the sky.

"Greetings, my child. I am Kali, fierce goddess of death and destruction. I can help you to cut down all that stands in your way. Bring me your issues, your beliefs that are holding you back. Come, let us face what is holding you captive. Take up my great sword and wield it well!"

Take up the great sword of Kali. Feel the power flowing in your veins, the strength moving through your body.

Bring your awareness to any issues that surface. They can be anything that has been an issue: something holding back advancement on your path forward, or maybe some beliefs that are keeping you stuck. Perhaps it's a relationship or something at work. These are the "demons" that haunt you.

As these demons swirl in your mind, take aim at them with the sword and say:

"Demons that haunt me and hold me back,
I will no longer be frozen by your lack.
With this blade I am now free,
As I will it, so shall it be."

Swing your blade at a demon and envision it being destroyed, shattered into a million pieces. Feel the weight of it being lifted. Repeat this for each demon.

"You can use my sword at any time to slay the demons. Know that you have the power to vanquish all that stands in your way."

Bring your attention back to your body, slowly open your eyes, and take a few deep breaths. As you step back into your day, take the guidance and messages of Kali with you.

KALI · WARRIORESS AND GREAT DESTROYER

Matters Associated with Kali

* Battle, war, revenge, protection, and destruction
* Taking action and control
* Reclaiming our voice and power
* Freedom, independence, and fighting oppression
* Embracing sexuality, lust, and passion
* Transformation, release, and change
* Facing darkness, fears, and obstacles
* Truth, strength, and courage
* Endings and beginnings
* Out-of-control anger and rage

Kali Affirmation

"I have the power to transform my life. I am courageous and can overcome my fears. I cut through all problems that arise. In the face of great change, I am fearless. I overcome all blocks on my path. I accept the endings that are needed to facilitate new beginnings. I embrace the wildness of my fierce feminine spirit. I am liberated from all that holds me back."

Kali Associations

CRYSTALS	Bloodstone, black tourmaline, black obsidian, smoky quartz, black kyanite, black onyx
COLORS	Black
PLANTS & OILS	Dragon's blood, patchouli, cypress, eucalyptus, spruce, birch, morning glory, ivy, Spanish moss, mimosa, asafoetida, bindweed, spikenard, yerba santa
ARCHETYPES	Warrioress. Dark Mother. Destroyer. The Wild Feminine. The Black Goddess.
SYMBOLS	Sword, skulls, tongue

HOWL: EMBODYING THE WARRIORESS

Kali is a mighty warrioress, the embodiment of the fierce feminine. Through her we can connect to this energy and become empowered. One way we can do this is by reclaiming our voice and movement.

Society has taught us that we need to be quiet and behaved, to keep our voices low and our movements "proper." This does not sit well with Kali. She reminds us that through powerful movements of the body and face, we derive great power.

Stand up and place your feet hip-distance apart, knees slightly bent. Bring your arms up from your body a few inches and bend your elbows slightly, hands pointed up and in claw shape. Stick your tongue out of your mouth, and as you do, release a short "HAA" sound a few times. If you feel called to, stomp your feet, alternating them, and pump your arms up and down. You can envision yourself "stomping" on demons with your feet, just as Kali did to vanquish the evil that plagued the world.

If you cannot stand, from a chair, bend your elbows and create the claw shape with your hands. Stick out your tongue and repeat the "HAA" sound. Pump your hands up and down.

By tapping into the wild energy of Kali in movement, we free ourselves of the expectations of behaving "perfectly."

DARK MOON FEAR-RELEASING RITUAL

The dark moon occurs the day and a half before and after the new moon, when there is no illumination by the sun. The dark moon marks the end of the previous cycle, the time when things are darkest and we go within our inner selves. This is the pause between the breaths. This is a time of stillness and of great healing. This dark moon is Kali's time, as she is connected to endings, the death of past cycles, and resurrection into what is becoming.

As we look toward the shadows that dwell within, we can face fears and uncertainty. The dark of the moon is the perfect time to cast aside these fears and move toward the new moon and the beginnings that come with a new cycle.

SUPPLIES

Black pen or marker

Piece of paper

Black candle and fireproof container or a bonfire

Natural offering, such as flower petals, herbs, birdseed, or crystals

Gather the items during the dark of the moon. Light the candle and say:

"Goddess Kali, on this dark night
I look inside with great insight.
I see the fears that hold me back,
The uncertainty, the wounds, and the lack.
Goddess Kali, help me see
What to let go so I am free."

With the pen and paper, write down all that you wish to let go of (for example, fears that have been present or relationships that need to be released). Take some time and list all that no longer serves your highest good.

When you are finished, fold up the list, envisioning your fears in one place. Set the paper on fire with the candle and let it burn in the fireproof container or bonfire. Picture all your fears and doubts being released, and say:

"Goddess Kali, hear my call.
Release what doesn't serve me at all.
As I burn away what doesn't fit me
In the light of this, I am now free."

When you are finished, take a few minutes and leave a natural offering to the Earth.

TIME DEVOURER INCANTATION

Kali is connected heavily with time. And, as the Great Devourer, she consumed demons to stop them from terrorizing the world. Her focus was unrelenting as she moved about the land devouring them.

Sometimes in our lives, many things get in the way and take up our time. This incantation can help to refocus our attention and stop letting time get away from us or get devoured by other things.

"To all that devours my time and energy,
I now bring the focus back toward me.
I cut all ties with all that is draining
Or anything that has my interest waning."

Envision taking up Kali's mighty sword and cutting away all the things that consume unnecessary energy or time in your life. Imagine it being severed from you and floating away.

SEEDS OF RENEWAL

Within Kali's arms of destruction, we find the perfect new soil for renewal and rebirth. This practice is for when we are opening to the new beginnings that occur after great change. Do this practice during the dark or new moon. If you feel called to plant something that will grow, you can plant seeds to tend.

SUPPLIES

Pot and soil, or an outdoor location
Spade
Seeds or a natural item, such as an acorn or pinecone, to bury

Gather the supplies. Hold what you wish to bury and infuse it with your intention or desire. You can also hold the general intention for new beginnings. Bury your seed or natural item in the soil and say:

"Goddess Kali, Lady of the Dark,
I plant what I desire in this soil so stark.
As all things begin in the great unknown,
May renewal occur for what I have sown.
Let my desires come to be.
As I will it, so shall it be."

3

ARADIA

QUEEN OF WITCHES

· · · · · · · · · · · · · · · · ● ● ● · · · · · · · · · · · · · · · ·

THE WITCH

THE MOON GODDESS

THE PILGRIM

DAUGHTER OF DIANA

THE WANDERESS

QUEEN OF WITCHES

· · · · · · · · · · · · · · · · ● ● ● · · · · · · · · · · · · · · · ·

Aradia is a powerful goddess often connected
with *Stregheria*, or "the Old Religion," in Italy.
She is called Queen of Witches and thought to be
a moon goddess, daughter of the great goddess
Diana and the light bearer Lucifer, as told in
Charles Leland's *Aradia: Gospel of Witches.*

ARADIA INVOCATION

"Goddess Aradia, witch and Lady of the Moon, I dedicate myself to your wisdom and to your guidance in the old ways. May you illuminate the dark corners of injustice that plague this world and show me how to stand up for all that I believe in. Shine a light on the ancient wisdom that flows within me so I, too, can reclaim my birthright as witch."

ARADIA was sent down to earth by her mother, Diana, to teach those who were oppressed the ways of the witch. She sought to liberate them from the tyranny of their persecutors as the living incarnation of her mother. Her name translates to "goddess of the altar" or "altar of the goddess," which could be referring to her followers worshiping her mother Diana through her. Ara (altar) is a constellation in the night sky that was placed upside down so her flame of wisdom could be cast down upon the world. *Dia* translates to "divine" in ancient Greek.

In another myth, Aradia was born into an Italian family, and she had a deep connection to the spiritual realm. Her family thought that she would become a nun, but that was not to be. Her beliefs lay elsewhere, in the wisdom of the full moon. Within her soul lies the knowledge of the forgotten gods, the medicine of the herbs, and the mystery of the earth. She heard the voice of the planet and of the spirits. In her human form, some believe that she was a reincarnation of the goddess Aradia.

Many feared Aradia as she worked her magick in the forest, and was often apprehended and jailed because of her beliefs. She would always escape, living to work her magick another day. *La Bella Pellegrina*, "the beautiful pilgrim," as she was called, taught the wisdom of the Old Religion to the people she met along her journey.

Aradia is said to have been born on August 13, 1313, and initiated into the Old Religion on her thirteenth birthday. When she was locked up, trapped by her parents and the priests for her beliefs, her lover liberated her. They escaped into the forest, so she could teach her wild wisdom to the world. She was said to appear to her followers in disguise. She taught them the old ways and the whispers of the earth, the secrets of the plants that could be used to protect and heal.

Aradia is powerful to work with during times of oppression. She is a hands-on goddess who connects us with our divine power to work sacred rites of protection, healing, and manifestation. Aradia can teach you to reclaim your voice, to not back down, and to connect with the medicine that lies hidden in the natural world.

RECLAIMING THE WITCH

The goddess Aradia brought the teachings of the old ways to the common people, but she was persecuted for it and went underground. After all, the word *witch* has been under sharp scrutiny and misrepresented for generations, by those who feared the ancient wisdom associated with it. In this practice, we connect with Aradia to reclaim our ancient birthright as witch.

Lie down in a safe, comfortable place and take a few deep, centering breaths. Close your eyes and relax your body.

Find yourself in a grotto, surrounded by fragrant trees and plants. The full moon shines brightly in the night sky. You see smoke rising from a fire, a cauldron bubbling atop the flames, and Aradia standing by the fire, adding herbs to the pot.

"Welcome to my sacred fire. I am Aradia, Queen of the Witches. They tried to take the sacred words, our ancient birthright, from us, attempted to steal the magic from our bones. But they can't. The great wisdom of the old ones is etched upon you, and it will never be erased."

Aradia holds her hands up to the moonlight, gathering the rays in her palms.

"Like the witches of old, we too find power and medicine in the light of the moon. Here we connect with the ancient ways. Come, connect if it is your will."

Hold your hands up to the moonlight and feel the ancient wisdom flow through your fingers. You feel at peace, connected to the thread of divine wisdom that is woven within your soul as you draw down the powerful lunar energy. Feel the wisdom of the goddess Aradia flowing through you, healing you, and offering you insight and clarity where you need it in your life.

"As you walk in this world, take the knowledge of the ancients with you, knowing that it flows within you always. You can draw down the power of the moon and connect with its magick whenever you feel called."

Bring your attention back to your body, slowly open your eyes, and take a few deep breaths. As you step back into your day, take the guidance and messages of Aradia with you.

Matters Associated with Aradia

* Moon magic, especially the full moon
* Learning the old ways and rituals
* Protection
* Divination
* Manifestation
* Ancient knowledge and wisdom
* Working our magic in private
* Fighting back against oppression

Aradia Affirmation

"I honor the magick that flows within me. I embrace the truth of all that I am. I open myself to the medicine that I am here to bring into the world. I connect with the ancient wisdom of the moon and tap into her deepest insight."

Aradia Associations

CRYSTALS	Auralite 23, garnet, moonstone, selenite
COLORS	Red, purple, white
PLANTS & OILS	Rue, vervain, verbena, nettle, mugwort, wormwood (poisonous)
ARCHETYPES	The Witch. The Moon Goddess. The Pilgrim. Daughter of Diana. The Wanderess. Queen of Witches.
SYMBOLS	Full moon, red garter, crescent moon

DIVINATION BY THE FULL MOON (WATER SCRYING)

The full moon offers us illumination into the unseen. Scrying using a bowl of water and the full moon's light can be a powerful divination tool for tapping into our deeper intuition. The goddess Aradia asked her followers to call upon her during the time of the full moon, so this is a potent practice to use with her magick.

SUPPLIES
Dark bowl
Water to fill the bowl

Fill your bowl with water. Go outdoors, if possible, on the night of the full moon. You can also do this indoors in the light of the moon. If you have a specific question, set your intention before you begin scrying. If not, be open to what will be revealed. Allow the bowl of water to sit charging in the moonlight. Take some time to relax and ease your body. Focus your eyes on the water and allow your mind to wander. Try not to control your thoughts or the images that rise; let them move and shift naturally. When you are finished, thank the moon for illumination and insight. Pay attention to the messages that flow after the ritual ends. Dreams can continue to reveal wisdom to you. After, use the water as charged lunar water or you can use it as an offering to the goddess in your garden, in your house plants, or anywhere outside.

    NOTE: If the moon is not out, you can light candles to help in illumination. The power of the full moon is still present.

CHARGING BY THE MOONLIGHT (LUNAR CHARGING)

The light of the full moon is a powerful tool for charging and clearing. It can energize and cleanse sacred items, such as crystals that can hold negative vibration. Some stones are sensitive to other methods of cleansing, such as water or sunlight, so a moon bath is the perfect way to clear them. Items such as as tarot cards, art supplies, and jewelry, can also benefit from a cleansing to release any absorbed energy.

SUPPLIES
Items you wish to charge or clear: crystals, tarot cards, art supplies, jewelry, etc.
Full moon

Place your items in the moonlight. They can be outdoors or on a windowsill indoors. If the moon is covered you can still set out the items. The energy of the moon reaches us at an internal level and can shift our behavior—it has the power to reach your items through clouds. You can clear and charge items monthly with the full moon. You can also add an intention by holding the item to be charged and say, "I am inspired with creativity" for art supplies or "I am filled with truth and clarity" for divination tools.

When you are finished, offer thanks to the full moon for her blessings:

"Goddess of the moon, I thank thee for your boon.
Bless me this night, and bless my sacred rite.
Carry me in favor and in your divine sight."

SEAL AN ENEMY

At times, people in our lives need to be stopped from causing us intentional harm. This wax seal can stop an enemy.

SUPPLIES
Candle
Paper and pen
Pin
Pepper or a dark herb, such as nettle or thistle

Gather your items and light the candle. Write your enemy's name on the paper. Fold the paper, trapping the name inside. Pour the wax on the paper, sealing it closed. While the wax is still pliable, use the pin to mark it with an X. Sprinkle the pepper or herbs on the wax. Envision your enemy being sealed, no longer able to bother you or cause you harm.

"Enemy of mine, your face I see.
No more will you bother me.
You are now sealed; you have no power.
You will leave me be from this very hour.
Lady Aradia, goddess of the witch,
Let this seal take hold without a glitch.
Grant me your power to stop this permanently.
As I will it so shall it be."

When finished, burn the paper and scatter the ashes somewhere far away from you.

WITCH BAG

Witch bags are simple cloth pouches that pack a powerful punch. Filled with herbs, crystals, and intentions, they are potent tools for drawing or repelling what we wish. These simple charms have been used for centuries as a way of working one's desires.

SUPPLIES

4 inch × 4 inch (10 cm × 10 cm) cotton or linen fabric square (see below for color)
Candle (see below)
Small piece of paper and a pen
Herbs or crystals (see below)
Small mirror or reflective fragment (optional)
String
Cord to hang from neck

For drawing: To create a witch bag for attraction, choose a fabric color that is in alignment with your intention. You can also match the color of your candle to your intention and fabric. To draw love, use red or pink. For abundance, use green or gold. For harmony, healing, or peace, use blue. Use purple for divination. White can be substituted for any color. Create these witch bags during the waxing moon.

Herbs and crystals that can be used for these intentions are:
Love Rose quartz, pink calcite, basil, cinnamon, clove, rose
Abundance Citrine, green aventurine, rutilated quartz, fern, orange, cedar, ginger, wheat, rice
Peace Amethyst, celestite, lavender, violet

Light the candle. Write your intention on the paper. Fold it and place it in the middle of the fabric with herbs and crystals. Gather the edges together and tie with string. Carry it with you until you feel your desire has manifested then bury in the earth.

For repelling: Black is usually the color associated with repelling or banishing. You can also use a small mirror or reflective fragment to mirror back energy. Create these witch bags during the waning moon.

Herbs and crystals used to repel energy or banish are black tourmaline, black obsidian, labradorite, jet, black onyx, salt, pepper, chili pepper, thistle, burr, and rosemary.

Follow the same process as above to create the witch bag. Create your intention and fill the cloth. Carry it with you for as long as you feel the desire for added protection, and then bury it when no longer needed.

4

PERSEPHONE

THE DARK QUEEN

GODDESS OF SPRING

MAIDEN

QUEEN OF THE UNDERWORLD

DARK GODDESS

Persephone is a goddess of many faces.
In her incarnation as Kore, she is the Goddess
of Spring and depicted as an innocent maiden.
As Persephone, she embodies the queen of the
underworld and dark goddess.

PERSEPHONE INVOCATION

"Lady of light and dark, spring and death, grant me the grace to open to the cycles that flow within my life. All things transform, even time spent in the shadows. I acknowledge the ancient wisdom of the crone that swims within my veins and the innocence of the maiden that keeps me curious to my deeper mystery. From you, Persephone, I learn I can be all things: wise woman, gentle heart, and dark queen."

IN most Persephone myths, she was portrayed as a naïve maiden who was kidnapped by the dark god of the underworld, Hades. This sent her mother Demeter, goddess of the grain, into a grief spiral that killed all the plants. Everyone began to starve and the world was in great peril. This causes other gods to intervene and tell Hades to let Persephone return to her mother. However, in the underworld is if you eat what grows there, you are not allowed to leave. Persephone ate six pomegranate seeds while in the underworld and thus must return for six months of the year. During this time, winter falls on the land of the living. When she returns from the underworld, the land flourishes once more.

This tale usually depicts Hades, as an oppressive force with no regard for the will of others. However, in the myth of Persephone, I see a maiden being reborn, becoming a queen in her own right.

I interpret the Persephone myth as the story of a woman looking to live her own life, to follow her own path in alignment with her heart, and to balance that with a mother having great difficulty in letting her daughter go. While her mother's intentions are to protect her child, they take away from her daughter's free will. Persephone was not a victim but a willing participant in her own destiny, moving from the spring of her life (childhood) toward her fullest power and deepest truth (queen) by embracing her dark aspects in the underworld.

Persephone is a powerful goddess, as she is indicative of birth, innocence, death, and rebirth. She embodies aspects of maiden, mother, and crone in her voyage to maturity. As we tap into her energy, we see the cycles of the seasons in nature as well as in our own lives. She shows us that we too can shift with the changes of the wheel of the year and flow with transformation. She teaches us that sometimes the path in front of us may be dark, but when we honor our truth, all things are illuminated in the end. She tells us that we, too, can be both light and dark.

THE QUEEN'S THRONE—RECLAIMING OUR PATH

Persephone goes through great transformation on her path from goddess of spring to queen of the underworld. She leaves behind her mother's expectations and taps into her sovereignty and power. Persephone can help us walk our own embodied path.

Lie down in a safe, comfortable place and take a few deep, centering breaths. Close your eyes and relax your body.

Envision yourself standing in a beautiful setting, surrounded by lush grasses, spring flowers, and swaying trees. Everything around you bursts with life. Follow the path toward the goddess Persephone, who stands before you wearing a regal crown.

"Greetings, and welcome to my garden. This is the place where I first dwelled when I was the embodiment of the goddess of spring, Kore. Here is where my myth began."

She motions to follow her as she walks through the garden.

"Spring is the beginning of all things, unblemished and sweet in nature, bursting with promise. It is much the same with people, who are full of potential and possibility. But some would keep us here, wrapped in a veil of innocence and naivete, away from the eyes of the world, as did my mother, Demeter. All mothers want to hold their children in a place of safety, away from the harsh reality of the world. But we, too, must walk our own sacred path, reclaiming our truth and our purpose on the planet away from the expectations of others."

You reach the end of the floral path and stand at the gates of the underworld.

"The truth is, one must enter the underworld willingly, as we must give ourselves over to seeing the shadows that dwell within us. You can be led to the gate, but you must enter of your own volition; no one can force you. I entered the darkness willingly, and that is a choice that we all make. I embraced my shadow, and now the time has come for you to look within and do the same. To rule your world sovereign and centered in your deepest truth, you need to embrace all aspects of your being. Do you willingly embrace yourself, darkness and light, and enter the unknown lands of your own free will?"

Give your answer to Persephone.

"If it is your will, follow me now through the gates."

Matters Associated with Persephone

* Moving through cycles, change, and transformation
* Separating from a person or place
* Rebirth, spring, and renewal
* Innocence of the Maiden
* Wisdom of the Crone
* Agriculture
* Death, the underworld, and the afterlife
* Dark night of the soul
* Longing of the soul

Persephone Affirmation

"I honor the cycles that flow in my life. I open to the transformation that occurs. I know that with each death comes rebirth into something new. I embrace my darkness and my light. I am whole. I honor my truth and follow my own path."

Persephone Associations

CRYSTALS	Garnet, ruby
COLORS	Gray, silver, black, garnet red (Persephone aspects), spring and pastel colors (Kore aspect)
PLANTS & OILS	Fir, willow, cedarwood, cherry, cypress, parsley, pine, poppy, vervain, verbena, vetiver, wintergreen
ARCHETYPES	Goddess of Spring. Maiden. Queen of the Underworld. Dark Goddess.
SYMBOLS	Pomegranate, spring flowers, grain, seeds

Follow Persephone through the gates of the underworld. Notice that the walls are glittering crystals from the depths of the earth, and their luminescence reflects the torchlight. An ethereal glow transcends the darkness. Persephone motions to a throne in the middle of the room. On the throne sits a crown.

> *"The underworld is rarely what others believe it to be. This is a place of truth, illumination, hope, and coming home to ourselves. The time has come to take up your crown and rule from a place of wholeness, away from the expectations of others. You can be all things, as I am both the goddess of spring and of darkness. Let no one define your fire or how you embody your truth."*

Walk to the throne and place the crown on your head. Sit down on the throne, knowing that you are walking your own path free from the expectations of others.

> *"I bow to you, queen and sovereign of your own life. Never let them take your crown from you."*

Bring your attention back to your body, slowly open your eyes, and take a few deep breaths. As you step back into your day, take Persephone's guidance and messages with you.

SPEAKING TO THE MAIDEN

The goddess Persephone embodies the maiden who evolves and embraces her wisdom, shadow, and wholeness in her transformation to queen of the underworld. In this practice, we connect with the energy of our inner child, acknowledging and recognizing past pain, hurt, and wounds.

SUPPLIES
Childhood photo of yourself

Find a place where you will be undisturbed. Get comfortable and hold the photo in your hands. Take some time to study it and connect with the feelings that come up. What surfaces may be difficult but try to remain present to observe what rises. Take a few minutes and speak kindly to your child-self. Confide in them, tell the child your pain, your grief, and your hopes. Connect to the dreams that your child-self had, the things they wanted to do, and all the hopes present for you as a child.

Vow to your inner child that you will take the sparks that once ignited you with you into the future and reconnect with the desires you once had. When you are finished, thank your child-self for connecting with you. Place the photo somewhere you can see it often as a touchstone to your connection to the past and vow for the future.

BLESSING A LOVER

The relationship between Persephone and Hades will always be open for interpretation. But we do know that, as lovers often are, they are separated for six months each year when Persephone returns to the Earth as the goddess of spring. This blessing of protection and abundance can be offered to a lover when there is separation—or when you wish to honor your love, no matter where they are.

SUPPLIES
Candle

Light the candle and offer the blessing:

> *"Love of my heart, I bless thee*
> *With love and luck and prosperity.*
> *Whether I am by your side or away from your arms,*
> *May you be protected against all hurt and harms.*
> *Goddess Persephone, hear my plea.*
> *Visit your blessings upon my love and me."*

MIRROR, MIRROR SPELL REVERSAL

At times, we may feel we are the recipient of a negative spell. This ritual can help repel that energy away. It can be performed during the new moon or at sunset.

SUPPLIES
Salt water, dried herb bundle, or moon water (optional)
Small candle in a dark color; Salt; Small mirror, such as a compact mirror

Light the candle. Sprinkle some salt on the mirror to cleanse it. Take it in your hands. Envision it glowing with protective energy, and say:

> *"Mirror, mirror in my hand, protect me now where I stand.*
> *Reflect back all ill to who sent it forth*
> *From west to east, south to north.*
> *Shield me from all negativity.*
> *As I will it, so shall it be."*

Place the mirror where it won't be disturbed, facing away from you like a shield, in a window or by your bed. You can repeat this as often as needed to keep the mirror charged with your intention. If it is no longer needed, bury it outside facing away from your home.

WORLDS APART: LOVE INVOCATION DURING TIMES OF SEPARATION

There may be times when we are separated from the one we love by distance, circumstance, or time. When we are feeling the ache of longing for them, we can perform this ritual.

SUPPLIES
Red candle; 6 garnets, rubies, or other red stones; 6 pomegranate seeds
Container of earth

Place the candle on your altar and arrange the stones evenly spaced around it. Place the seeds between each stone, evenly spaced. Light the candle and say:

"To the one that I love
Who is not here with me,
Deep pain I feel
When your face I can't see.

The distance between us is vast.
The days without you are long.
No matter how many hours until I next see you
My heart remains strong.

Like Persephone,
I dwell in another world without you,
But only for a time.
This will not last.
Like winter turns to spring,
All things must pass.

Bury the pomegranate seeds in the dirt.

"As these seeds return
To the earth once more,
So too shall I return to your arms. So it is."

Keep the stones where you can see them. Focus on the love that connects you even though you are apart. You can also carry the stones with you for strength and support. Place the soil outside in the earth if you feel called to, envisioning your intentions flowing deep into the ground.

5

INANNA

THE QUEEN OF HEAVEN

· ● ·

QUEEN OF HEAVEN AND EARTH

GODDESS OF LOVE AND WAR

GODDESS OF THE GRAIN

· ● ·

Inanna is a powerful Sumerian goddess attributed most often to the aspects of love and war. She has been associated with Ishtar (the Mesopotamian goddess) and Aphrodite (the Greek goddess). Connected with both the morning star and the evening star, she is also known as the Queen of Heaven and Earth.

INANNA INVOCATION

"Goddess Inanna, Queen of Heaven and Earth, like you I have ventured into the underworld to see the darkest parts of myself and have returned triumphant. Grant me the strength to let go of the people and thoughts that no longer support the truth of my soul. May you bless my path forward, ever changing and ever evolving."

MANY myths surround Inanna, but the most popular is the story of her journey into the underworld to see her dark sister Ereshkigal, who reigns there as queen. In some versions of the myth, she is there for the funeral of her sister's husband, whom she sent into battle to his death. Along the journey, Inanna was asked to strip away all her brilliant robes and jewels. She gave up all that she has been taught defines her and faced her shadow in the darkness.

Ereshkigal was not happy at her sister's presence in her domain, and she proceeded to kill her and hang her corpse on a hook. There she stayed for three days and nights. After three days, Inanna's priestess Ninshubar, who has been waiting for her return, set to beating her drum in mourning and to petition for Inanna's release back to the land of the living. Ninshubar asked for aid from Enki, the god of wisdom and water, who sent spirits to trick Ereshkigal and sprinkle Inanna with water of life. She was reborn back into the world by her shadow self, Ereshkigal, symbolizing her coming into her complete power. But she was only allowed to leave on the condition that someone replaced her in the underworld. Ereshkigal suggested Ninshubar, which Inanna refused. She will not give up her loyal priestess who beat the drum from her and came to her aid.

She returned to the earth to search out a suitable replacement. There she found that in her absence, her husband, Dumuzi, did not mourn her absence, but instead consorted with other women, held celebrations, and ruled from her throne in an attempt to secure his own kingship over her land. So, Inanna offered him up to the Queen of the Underworld to take her place. Dumuzi's sister Gestinanna, however, begged Inanna to free him. Inanna partly agreed, with the condition that Gestinanna agreed to takes his place for six months of the year. As Dumuzi was an agricultural god, this is another telling of the origin of winter/spring season, during which there is death of vegetation and the world enters a time of rest.

The story of Inanna shows us the power of merging the aspects of light and dark to rule from a place of wholeness. When Inanna embraced her darkness and her light, she could go back to her realm and rule from a solid foundation. In the story of Dumuzi, we see the price of betrayal and learn that sometimes you have to leave behind those who are not in your corner. Inanna tells us that we can reign sovereign over our own lives. She is symbolic of death, rebirth, and embracing the truth that flows in our veins so we can rule our lives from a place of truth and authenticity on our own.

VISUALIZATION

JOURNEY INTO DARKNESS—THE ALTAR OF INANNA

On her journey into the underworld, the goddess Inanna had to lay down everything that she had been taught defined her. She ventured away from the safety of her own realm, where she ruled as queen, and met with her shadow in the underworld. Inanna can help us to release the aspects of ourselves that we have been taught we need to uphold because others or society have told us that we should.

Lie down in a safe, comfortable place and take a few deep, centering breaths. Close your eyes and relax your body.

You find yourself in a beautiful palace, the spires of its towers stretching high toward the sky. Banners hang from the gilded walls and flutter in the breeze. A woman with a crown on her regal head walks toward you.

"I am Inanna, Queen of Heaven and Earth. This is my realm, and here I rule connected with my deepest truth. But it was not always so. Once I ruled from a place that others had dictated for me. I reveled in the trappings that I was taught must define me. It was only when I gave up the things I thought I needed that I was able to face all aspects of myself and become wholly centered in my purpose. The time has come for you to do the same, to let go of what no longer serves you in order to resonate with the truth of all that you are."

Inanna walks the pathway from the palace toward a gate in the distance. Walk with her. When you reach the gate, there is an altar placed before it. Standing beside it is Inanna's loyal priestess Ninshubar, drumming on her sacred drum.

"This is the altar on which we must sacrifice the old versions of ourselves that no longer fit. When I journeyed to the underworld, I let go of everything— my crown, my jewels, even the husband who had no grief for me when I was gone. All of these things were supposed to define me, but I had outgrown them all and they were weighing me down. What do you wish to leave behind on the altar?"

Take a few minutes to think of what you wish to leave behind. This can be anything from relationships to fears to old jobs. As you resonate with something you wish to

Matters Associated with Inanna

* Transformation
* Letting go of the past
* Moving from light to darkness
* Embodying wholeness
* Facing our shadows
* Leaving unhealthy relationships
* Embracing darkness and light
* Sensuality and sacred sexuality
* Leading from a place of authenticity
* Loyalty
* Sisterhood
* Friendship

Inanna Affirmation

"I embrace my darkness and my light. I embody all aspects of my being. I resonate with the truth of my soul. I follow my own path. I let go of all that no longer serves me or my highest good. I walk forward rooted in my wholeness. I am complete. I am queen of my own life."

Inanna Associations

CRYSTALS	Lapis lazuli
COLORS	Red, royal blue
PLANTS & OILS	Grain, seeds, reeds
ARCHETYPES	Queen of Heaven and Earth. Goddess of Love and War. Goddess of the Grain.
SYMBOLS	Lions, snakes, cattle, jackal, dove, swallow, raven, stars

let go of, place it on the altar of Inanna. Feel it being lifted from you, as it no longer embodies who you are. As your offerings are placed on the altar, Ninshubar drums and they begin to disappear.

> *"When we have lost it all and venture into the unknown, there is great power. Here you stand bare, free of the trappings that once bound you. Blessings to you on the path forward. Know that no matter what we are stripped of in this life, our truth remains."*

Bring your attention back to your body, slowly open your eyes, and take a few deep breaths. As you step back into your day, take Inanna's guidance and messages with you.

RELEASING A LOVER

When Inanna realized that her unsupportive husband, Dumuzi, didn't miss her when she went to the underworld and that he instead celebrated, she released him and gave him to the underworld. Sometimes we find ourselves faced with unsupportive partners and need to let them go. Practice this during a waning moon, on the new moon, or at sunset.

SUPPLIES
Smudge or moon water; Black candle; String or cord; Scissors or knife; Fire

Start by gathering anything and everything connected to the partner. It's a good idea to clear your space of any reminders of them and any of their possessions. Smudge your home or spray moon water when you are finished to clear the energy.

When you have this accomplished, gather your items and light the candle. Take the cord in your fingers and say:

> *"What we had is now at an end.*
> *All that was is now through.*
> *As I cut this cord, there is no more me and you."*

Cut the cord, envisioning all connections between you ceasing.

> *"All ties between us are now cut.*
> *The door to this union is now closed shut.*
> *I call back all energetic ties to me.*
> *As I will it, so shall it be."*

Take the cords and burn them, symbolizing the end of the connection. When you are finished, snuff out the candle and say:

*"The connection of this union has been released.
It is over. It is done. Go in peace."*

WRITTEN IN THE HEAVENS: CALLING IN A PARTNER

Inanna is also a goddess of love. When she released her husband, Dumuzi, to the underworld, I think she would have opened herself up to a more authentic relationship in her new connection to her deepest truth, if she felt the desire to do so. You can do this practice on a Friday during a waxing moon.

SUPPLIES

Sacred fire or container fire (If you do not have access to a fire, you can place everything in a bowl and bury it when you are finished.)
Rose quartz
Red and pink candle (or substitute white)
Paper and pen
Cinnamon, thyme, lavender, rose, oak, sandalwood, or sage
Offering

Gather all the items near a sacred fire outdoors. Place the rose quartz between the two candles and light them. With your paper and pen, spend some time connecting with what you are looking for in a mate. Write all these thoughts down, and be specific. How you would embody such a connection. How does it feel?

When you are finished, sprinkle the herbs on the sacred fire. Then offer your list to the flames and say:

*"Goddess Inanna, queen of heaven,
Guide my love to me.
May they be my equal,
A true partner for me.
Goddess Inanna, bring my love to me."*

When you are finished, leave an offering and celebrate. If you added your items to a bowl, take them outside and bury them in the earth, offering your intentions to the soil.

THE PRIESTESS DRUM: SUPPORTING OUR SISTERS

When the goddess Inanna ventured into the underworld, her loyal priestess Ninshubar entreated the god Enki to save her beloved queen. She was the one who tirelessly beat the drum for her return, so dedicated was she to her friend and queen. In this way, we too can beat the drum of support for our sisters.

SUPPLIES

Pen and paper

Close your eyes and find your breath. Take a few minutes to ground and center. Connect with the drum beat of your heart.

With the pen and paper, craft a vow of sisterhood, one that details how you will support others. For example: *"I vow to give up gossiping about my fellow priestesses. I will help others rise and support their voices. We are all in this together."*

Take however long you need to connect to your Ninshubar energy, the energy of the loyal friend and priestess. If you feel called to deepen the practice, you can recite your vows while drumming.

OFF THE HOOK

In the story of Inanna venturing into the underworld, she gives up everything she thought had value and looks deep within herself to face her shadow and truth. After Ereshkigal kills her and hangs her on a hook, she gives up control and is reborn from her old self into full embodiment of her own truth. So too can we let ourselves off the hook from our old lives and embrace our path forward.

SUPPLIES

Thin strip of paper

Twist the paper strip to make a hook. Envision all the things you are on the hook for that you no longer wish to control or that you want to be free. As you do, say:

"I am off the hook.
The past is removed from me.
From this hook I am now free."

Burn the hook and bury the ashes to release the hooks of the past.

ERESHKIGAL

GODDESS OF THE UNDERWORLD

GODDESS OF THE DEAD

QUEEN OF THE UNDERWORLD

Ereshkigal is the Sumerian goddess of the dead and sister to Inanna, goddess of heaven. As the goddess of the underworld, she passes judgment on souls who enter her gates and rules the gloomy land where the souls of the dead are said to howl for eternity. She is the shadow sister to Inanna and embodies the darker aspects of the soul. Ereshkigal is the mirror of truth that Inanna faced when she arrived in the underworld.

ERESHKIGAL INVOCATION

"Ereshkigal, hidden sister beneath the earth, Goddess of the Underworld. Within you, I find strength, to free myself from judgment and false pretense. I adorn my sacred self with praise and step into my truth, wholly integrating shadow and light. I will not scorn myself for my darkness nor will I strike others down for their medicine. I dive into all aspects of myself, from grief to abandonment and sorrow. I walk fully in my own truth, seeing myself as worthy and whole."

ERESHKIGAL embodies many feelings that we are taught to keep hidden in the darkness, such as anger, envy, and fear. She was jealous of her sister Inanna, envious of her power, beauty, and queendom in the land of the living. Thus, when Inanna arrived in her domain, Ereshkigal struck her down out of anger and jealousy. She is also connected with abandonment, as she is often perceived as the solitary sister alone in the darkness while Inanna rules above. Through her, we can connect to our own fears and wounds surrounding the energy of abandonment, grief, and feelings of unworthiness.

Another version of the story of Ereshkigal and Inanna is that the Queen of Heaven was selfish and wanted everything for herself, including the realm of her sister below. Inanna sent Ereshkigal's husband, Gugulana, the Bull of Heaven, to destroy the land of Gilgamesh, who had spurned Inanna's advances, and Gugulana was killed. Inanna then ventured callously into the Underworld for the funeral, with no regard for her sister's grief for her husband. Ereshkigal judged Inanna and killed her for her actions. Inanna rose three days later as in the Inanna myth, but she was far less heroic than she is in her own tale. In this version, Ereshkigal is misunderstood and wronged, showing us that even shadow aspects can be misjudged. She suffered at the hands of her sister's thoughtless ploys and ended up a grieving widow.

Ereshkigal is the embodiment of the shadow aspects of the self we have been taught that we need to hide. We are told that we need to be digestible, easy to take, and not to make a fuss. But the goddess Ereshkigal shows us there is great power in our shadows. Although we need to see them fully, they can be a source of great power and transformation.

MIRROR OF ERESHKIGAL—EMBODIMENT OF OUR SHADOW

Myths of Ereshkigal portray her as both villain and victim. Her deepest truth is when the two are merged and we see the dark queen in all her power ruling from her place in the underworld. She teaches us that we, too, need to drop the judgment of ourselves and embrace all that we are.

Lie down in a safe, comfortable place and take a few deep, centering breaths. Close your eyes and relax your body.

You find yourself in front of a vast, towering palace gate, the arch stretching toward the darkness above. Everything around you is shrouded in shadow. The gate opens and a guard beckons to you. You walk up the pathway toward a throne, seated upon which is the goddess Ereshkigal.

"My child, welcome to the underworld. Here in this place of shadow, you can see the truth of yourself."

Ereshkigal motions toward a large, dark mirror standing beside her throne.

"When we look at ourselves with the eyes of truth instead of the eyes of judgment, we fully embrace all that we are. I did so when I let go of my anger and jealousy toward my sister Inanna and embraced the magic of all that I am. So often we are taught that there is no benefit in the darkness, that no medicine dwells here. I am here to tell you that there is great wisdom in our darkest shadows. Within this mirror, you will face your truth without judgment. We have been taught to be harsh with ourselves, and we need to move away from this. Pay attention to any criticisms that comes up for you, and be there with them. Sit with them as a sister would."

Face the mirror and scan your reflection. Notice any judgments that arise when facing yourself. Are you thinking negatively about any aspect of yourself? Are you judging yourself harshly or unfairly? Are there thoughts present to parts of yourself that have been called "dark" or have not been accepted by others? Has your inner monologue shifted to one of criticism?

Envision these dark parts of yourself, your shadow self, the parts that can be hard for us to accept at times. Perhaps we feel unlovable or there is something specific we judge harshly about ourselves. Take a few moments to ease the negative self-talk and move into a place of acceptance for all that you are. Let go of the feelings of needing to be anything other than what you are here in this breath. See yourself as whole in the mirror, a tapestry of light and dark, of brilliance and insecurity. Envision all the aspects of yourself fusing together, all parts becoming whole.

Matters Associated with Ereshkigal

* Death and rebirth
* Confronting our shadows
* Facing judgment
* Seeing all aspects of ourselves
* Dealing with abandonment
* Grief and sorrow

Ereshkigal Affirmation

"I embrace my shadow. I see the beauty in all facets of my sacred being. I look at myself with eyes of praise and leave behind all judgment. I know myself to be worthy. I find strength in my solitude. I express all my feelings, even the ones I have been taught I should hide. I am whole and magnificent."

Ereshkigal Associations

CRYSTALS	Black tourmaline, black obsidian, snowflake obsidian, labradorite, black kyanite
COLORS	Black
PLANTS & OILS	Birch, dragon's blood, ambergris, blessed thistle
ARCHETYPES	Goddess of the Dead. Queen of the Underworld.
SYMBOLS	Hook, bull, corpses, skulls, bones, snakes, scorpions, beings of the hidden earth, owl

"With time and practice, we can move into a place of embracing all that we are. Go now, connected in your wholeness."

Bring your attention back to your body, slowly open your eyes, and take a few deep breaths. As you step back into your day, take Ereshkigal's guidance and messages with you.

THE FORGOTTEN SHADOW SISTER: DEALING WITH ABANDONMENT

In some interpretations of her myth, Ereshkigal felt abandoned, left to reign in the darkness unseen. She felt that Inanna was selfish and spoiled, getting everything that she wanted. This led to anger and resentment, so when Inanna came down to the Underworld on her pilgrimage, Ereshkigal was furious and passed a harsh sentence on her. The shadow sister aspect is something that we all embody, as we can feel left behind by others or jealous of them. This is a practice for facing those feelings and being our own mirror into their wisdom.

SUPPLIES
Pen and paper (optional)
Mirror (optional)

Find a quiet place where you will not be disturbed. Take some time and reach into your feelings surrounding abandonment, worthiness, and jealousy of others. Why are you jealous? Of whom are you jealous? Do you feel left behind or abandoned? If so, by whom? And why? If you are called to, write down your feelings as you explore them. This can be an intense journey within, and it can bring up some very dark shadows. The purpose isn't to judge them but to dive deeper into their roots.

These shadows arise because of our own uncertainty and feelings of unworthiness. We are taught to believe that we lack something that would make us worthy. But this isn't true. Craft words of praise to speak into the mirror. This can be difficult at first, as we are conditioned not to speak kindly to ourselves. For example, say:

"Hello. I know I haven't been there for you as much as I should be, but I will try to be from now on. I acknowledge that you feel left behind, but you're not alone. You have me."

Be aware, as you move forward, when you slip into negative dialogue about yourself. Try to gently guide yourself back to a place of acceptance and limit self-judgment.

BANISHING RITUAL

During our lives, there will be times when we wish to banish something—energy, unwanted situations, or even people. Ereshkigal can help us, as she wished to banish her sister from her domain.

SUPPLIES
Paper and pen;
Salt and pepper

Write down what you wish to banish. Sprinkle the paper with salt and pepper and fold it away from yourself to contain it. Say:

"I now cast all evil away from me.
I banish this now; now I am free.
You shall no longer bother me.
As I will it, so shall it be."

Dispose of the paper far away from you and don't look back at it when you leave. You can burn it and dispose of the ashes or bury it in the earth. It is banished and behind you now.

BANISHING POWDER

You can use banishing powder anywhere you need protection or shielding, for example, around the perimeter of your home, near doorways, or near gates. It should be buried so no animal can have access to it. Make it during the dark of the moon a day before the new moon.

SUPPLIES
Salt; Ash; Burrs or thorns;
Black tourmaline, crushed; Sealable glass bottle or jar

Mix all the ingredients together in a bowl. Store the powder in a glass bottle or jar. Sprinkle it around the home or near doorways as desired. It can also be placed in closed bottles around the home.

You can make a quick banishing practice by sprinkling the powder on a paper written with what you wish to banish and saying:

"Ereshkigal, banish all ill intent sent my way.
Evil energy, away you must stay."

Burn all in a fire.

BINDING RITUAL

Sometimes we know the source of our issue or the person with ill intent toward us. For these instances, we can create a binding ritual that restricts the ill intent of someone specific. For this ritual, we use an item of identity or a personal item belonging to the person we are binding that contains their energy.

SUPPLIES
Black candle; Salt;
Rosemary; Paper and pen
Item of identity (optional)
Straw or grass; Black string

Gather your supplies. Light the candle and sprinkle salt and rosemary around it. Write down the name of the person with ill intent toward you. If you have a personal item of this person's, you can use a small piece of it for this ritual. Fold the name and item. Use the straw to fashion the shape of a person around the paper and item: First bind the straw for the torso and head, and then add a cross section for the arms. It doesn't need to be perfect. You can also tie the paper and item to the finished doll. When the straw doll is crafted, wrap it with the string, tying it up and envisioning the person causing you ill stopping their evil intentions. Say:

"I bind you, _____, from causing harm to me and to those I love.
I bind your ill intents and negative eye.
I bind you from all vile intent."

If you do not have straw or grass to fashion the doll, you can simply write the person's name on the paper or on their item and bind that.

When you have finished, burn your chosen effigy and dispose of the ash somewhere else. Say:

"As my will is spoken, so your ill is broken.
You are bound from causing harm to me and harm to others.
Go your own way; leave me be.
As I will it, so shall it be."

MEDEINA

GODDESS OF THE WILD WOOD

THE WILD GODDESS

GODDESS OF THE HUNT

PROTECTRESS OF THE FOREST AND ANIMALS

EARTH WITCH

Medeina is from Lithuania; a goddess of the Baltic area. Connected with the wild wood, she was a huntress who was depicted as a beautiful maiden. She sometimes transformed herself into a wolf or was surrounded by a pack of wolves, and she could also be seen riding naked on a bear. She was said to play tricks on huntsmen or loggers in the woods, often leading them astray with her wild hare if she felt they were not honoring the animals or vegetation in the forest. She was not there to help humans; she was there to protect the forest and the life in it.

MEDEINA INVOCATION

"Medeina, goddess of the wild wood, embodiment of the wild feminine.
May I honor the fierce, untamed wilderness that flows within my veins, paying
homage to the ancient line of ferocious women who have come before me.
May I be as renewed as the Earth, ever changing and ever evolving, as I move
toward my deepest truth. I am unbreakable. I bend like the willow and am
strong as the oak. May your protection be granted to all animals and wild
places so that they may thrive. May I continue your dedication as a steward
of the Earth."

ANIMALS were sacred to Medeina, and her symbol was the wild hare. Although she was said to be beautiful and much sought after by suitors, she was unwilling to marry, preferring instead to run feral through the trees with her animal friends and craft potions in her forest home. As forest mother, she has little care for the intentions of humans and vowed to protect the Earth from their destruction. She would stop at nothing to protect the wild places from those who would do them harm.

The energy of Medeina is sometimes associated with that of Artemis and Diana, as they were also known as huntress goddesses and protectresses of the forest. Medeina's feral nature is connected to the archetype of the Wild Woman, and she reminds us of our home in the natural world and our duty to protect it. She connects us with the Wild Woman aspect within ourselves, allowing the untamed spirit that flows within to be set free. Howl, she tells us. Run free through the trees. Here you will find your power and your peace.

The goddess Medeina brings us the message of needing to connect deeper with the energy of the Earth and the medicine of the animals. She reminds us that it's our job to offer protection and reverence to these sacred places and beings. She tells us to celebrate our single selves and that we don't need a partner to be complete; we are whole on our own in the arms of all that we love and in our sacred purpose on this planet.

PROTECTION OF THE WILD WOOD

As goddess of the wild wood, Medeina connects us with the energy of the forest animals and the protection they bring

Lie down in a safe, comfortable place and take a few deep, centering breaths. Close your eyes and relax your body.

Envision yourself standing in a vast forest, ancient trees towering overhead. The full moon illuminates the evergreens and lends an ethereal glow to the world. An owl hoots from somewhere in the forest. Step forward onto the moss-covered path leading into the trees. Walk forward over the lush ground, the scents of earth filling the air. You come to a clearing where the goddess Medeina is standing in front of you.

"Welcome to the wild wood. Here you will find great solace. Many venture here during times of hardship seeking the protection of the trees and animals that dwell here. Have you come seeking the protection of the forest?"

Give the goddess your reply. She beckons you to stand in the middle of the clearing.

"May the protection of the forest be granted to you, this day and all days, as you stand in reverence to her power and beauty."

Stand in the middle of the clearing, feeling the magick of the forest surrounding you.

"Root yourself deeply in the forest. As you connect to the earth, so she will protect you."

Plant your feet firmly on the ground and feel the solid earth beneath you, supporting your foundation. You hear a howl in the night air, and out of the trees emerge thirteen wolves of various sizes and hues.

"These are the embodiment of the Earth, the sacred wolves of the goddess Medeina. They offer you the protection of the forest."

The wolves circle around you, guarding you with their presence. Let yourself feel a deep sense of safety resonating through your being.

Matters Associated with Medeina

* Earth medicine
* Protection of the natural world
* Connection with the cycles of the Earth
* Planetary wisdom
* Grounding
* Rebirth and renewal
* Healing using Earth practices
* Animal medicine and healing
* Thriving on our own

Medeina Affirmation

"I am open to the abundance of the Earth. I honor the natural world and its medicine. I find deep healing in the goddess's creations. I protect the wilderness and the animals. I am one with the world around me. I am blessed by the Earth."

Medeina Associations

CRYSTALS	Dravite, moss agate, smoky quartz, petrified wood, amber
COLORS	Green, brown
PLANTS & OILS	Cypress, vetiver, pine, birch, patchouli, bay, wild plants, ferns, trees
ARCHETYPES	The Wild Goddess. Goddess of the Hunt. Earth Witch. Protectress of the Forest and Animals.
SYMBOLS	Wolves, hares, forest, trees, leaves, ferns, paw prints, animal tracks

"The wolves of the forest are always there to protect you. Their energy travels with you each day. The forest can also heal you of what you wish to give up, swallowing your sorrow and your hardship. If there is something you wish to lay down, speak it now within this sacred circle and offer it to the ground."

If there is anything that you wish to let go of, speak it aloud to Medeina and the circle of wolves.

"May the Earth absorb what you wish to release. May you be blessed with wholeness and peace."

Bring your attention back to your body, slowly open your eyes, and take a few deep breaths. As you step back into your day, take Medeina's guidance and messages with you.

GROUNDING PRACTICE

Grounding is a way of connecting with the Earth and the self in order to come back to the present moment. Often, we become scattered in our daily lives and we need to take the time to come back to our breath in the moment. It is also a good idea to do some grounding before any other practice, as it can center our energy and bring us deeper clarity and focus.

VARIATION 1

Sit on the earth in the lotus position or cross-legged. If you can't sit directly on the earth, you can do this in your home. To further connect to the element of earth, you can hold a crystal, sit near plants, or incorporate the earth's grounding energy in your own way. Sit up straight and make sure your sit bones (butt bones) are touching the ground.

Place your palms face-up on your knees. Breath at a comfortable, sustainable pace. As you breathe in and out, envision your body rooted solidly to the earth below. Picture strong roots moving down through the soil and into the ground.

As you tap into this energy that connects you to the earth, feel it centering you, offering you solid foundation and support. Feel the nourishing energy of the earth flowing through you and anchoring you here in the present moment.

When you are finished, thank the earth for its grounding energy and pull the roots back to you, knowing you can connect again any time. Take the grounding energy with you throughout your day.

VARIATION 2

Use the yoga pose Mountain Pose or *Tadasana*. Begin with your feet hip-distance apart. Ground down through the soles of your feet and move your arms up over your head with your fingers touching in a peak where they meet. Follow the same rooting practice as above, but this time through your feet, envisioning a strong mountain that withstands all of life's winds.

You can also recite a grounding affirmation as you do these poses:

"I am firmly grounded.
I am safe and secure.
I am rooted deeply in my truth and in my purpose.
I connect with the energy of the Earth.
I release fear and uncertainty."

WASH AWAY THE MUCK

When an accumulation of muck sticks to the surface of our lives, it is time to remove it. Medeina is a goddess of the earth, and so with her we can connect with the clearing and purifying energy of the natural world.

SUPPLIES

Mud

Water

A place to get dirty

Envision what you want to wash away. It can be a situation, an obstacle, or anything that you wish to remove from your life. Use the mud to form an embodiment of it. You can form it into a totem of what you want to wash away if the mud is hard enough, or you can paint it like a sigil onto a rock or any hard surface that can withstand moisture.

When you have created your symbol, say:

"Away, away, wash away
All that stands in my way.
I release, I let go.
From me now you must flow.
Go from me, I am now free.
As I will it, so shall it be."

Now wash away the mud. If you can't do this outdoors, you can do it in your bathtub or sink with some fine mud and the shower hose, but be careful not to clog the drains. As you rinse away the muck, envision what you want to leave flowing away from your life.

EARTH WITCH BOTTLE TO ABSORB NEGATIVE ENERGY

Medeina was known as a powerful Earth witch, connecting with the energy of the natural world to heal and dispel negativity. Witch bottles are powerful talismans that can be filled with items to protect and to repel energy. This witch bottle is for when we wish to dispose of negative energies. This practice can be done on the new moon.

SUPPLIES

Sealable bottle or jar
Cotton balls
Salt
Vinegar

Gather the items and put the cotton, salt, and vinegar in the jar. Place it somewhere near the negative energy or in a general location near an entranceway to trap anything coming into the dwelling, whether it is a workplace, home, or somewhere else. Say:

"Goddess Medeina, protectress of the wild wood,
So, too, do I need your protection.
Absorb all ill and negativity sent my way.
Trap it and seal it and make it go away."

Leave it there for one moon cycle, until the next new moon, and then bury it far away from you and say:

"I send this energy far from me.
Away from my life it now will be.
I am surrounded by safety and security.
So it is; blessed be."

PROSPERITY AND ABUNDANCE RITUAL

The Earth is an abundant resource for us all. Medeina reminds us we can open ourselves to the energy of abundance and prosperity that flow through the natural world.

SUPPLIES

Earth items that symbolize abundance and plenty, such as pinecones, wheat, grains, acorns, flowers, or produce
Coins
Crystals, such as citrine, green aventurine, jade, and rutilated quartz
Bowl
Green candle

Dedicate a place in your home to your abundance and prosperity items where they won't be disturbed. Surround the candle with the coins and crystals. Light the candle and drop the natural items into the bowl as you say:

> *"I am a beacon to which prosperity is flowing.*
> *My abundance is expanding and ever growing."*

Envision the abundance of the Earth being drawn to you like a beacon. Spend some time thinking on how abundance looks in your life and what you wish to further manifest. Picture all these things coming to you as though drawn to a magnet. Let the candle burn down. When it is extinguished, take the natural items from the bowl and offer them to the Earth:

> *"As I nourish the Earth, so it nourishes me.*
> *With abundance, luck, and prosperity.*
> *All things good flow to me.*
> *As I will it, so shall it be."*

Leave the crystals and coins on your altar space, if you wish. You may also put them somewhere you can see them or carry them with you.

OYA

GODDESS OF STORMS

· · · · · · · · · · · · · · · · · · · ● ● ● · · · · · · · · · · · · · · · · · · ·

SHAPER OF STORMS

GODDESS OF WEATHER

FIRE GODDESS

· · · · · · · · · · · · · · · · · · · ● ● ● · · · · · · · · · · · · · · · · · · ·

Oya is the Yoruban goddess of weather and storms.
She is a multifaceted goddess, as she can be found in
the slightest breeze or the wildest of storms. She is known as
a champion who protects women during times of hardship,
poverty, and stress. She brings about great transformation
and carries with her a mighty sword, which she uses to cut
away what no longer serves the highest good, releasing the
past so something better can come in. Oya is also connected to
marketplaces and commerce, spellcraft, death, rebirth, and fire.

OYA INVOCATION

"Oya, goddess of transformation and shaper of storms, may your powerful winds blow into my life and clear away the stagnant and old. Let your winds scatter away the past that no longer fits and the ties that are no longer meant for me. Sweep clear the oppression of women and the tyranny of the oppressors. May your winds of change flow through my life and wipe the slate clean. May your blessings follow with abundance and joy. Oh Oya, mother of storms, give me the strength to walk the changes of my life."

OYA is passionate, fierce, and changeable, embodying the nature of storms and the earth. With her warrior fire energy, she is a protectress of women, their defender from tyranny, oppression, and suffering. Women pray to her to intercede on their behalf when they need a powerful force of reckoning after being put upon by others.

As she has the power to shape storms and turbulent weather, so she has the power to aid us as we deal with transformation in our own lives. Oya is a force of nature who can help us sweep away aspects that remain stuck. In this way, she is like a cosmic reset button, wiping the slate clean. Her energy can be erratic, showing us that sudden change may not be smooth.

Oya connects us with the primal and passionate feminine, shaking loose rules or chains placed upon her. She breaks free of "should," and, with a shake of her hips, she moves mountains. She reminds us to connect with the primal within ourselves and not to leave it caged because of the misunderstanding of others.

Oya moves in both the seen and unseen, traveling in the hidden realms of the Earth and guiding deep change into our world.

SEVERING THE PAST, MAKING WAY FOR THE FUTURE

At times in our lives, we need to clear away what no longer is meant for us, so we can call in something that fits us better. The goddess Oya, with her sword held high, cutting a pathway through the old to make room for the new , can guide us to make these sweeping changes.

Lie down in a safe, comfortable place and take a few deep, centering breaths. Close your eyes and relax your body.

You find yourself standing in a vast field, the skies above clear and blue. The field around you sways in the slight breeze, the grasses brushing your body as you walk through them. In the middle of the field, you see a woman with wild hair and eyes, and brandishing two swords in her hands.

"I am the goddess Oya, bringer of storms and transformation. I am the power that can help you to clear away the old to make way for the new."

She raises her swords to the sky and thunder rumbles in the distance. The sky darkens as clouds begin to gather.

"With our swords, we will clear a pathway into the future. Do not fear the changes that come with transformation, as they are needed to make room for what your heart is calling to you. Envision all the things that you need to cut from your life, all that you wish to release. Take this sword and raise it with me."

Take one sword from Oya and raise it to the lightning-filled sky. Envision what you wish to cut away from your life. Oya brings down the sharp blade of her own sword toward the field and cuts into the grain.

"Fall what is done, fall the complete,
Leave now, all that is over, delete, delete.
Renew, renew, we invite in the new.
We open this space to bring our desires into view.
As we sever the past, we make way for the future."

Walk along with Oya, bringing your sword to the grain and cutting a pathway through it, envisioning cutting down the obstacles in your own life and walking forward in their wake. When you get to the end of the field, Oya motions back to the path you cut through.

Matters Associated with Oya

* Connection to weather or storms
* Quick change and transformation
* Sweeping things clean
* Cosmic reset
* Blessing a business
* Pushing back against oppression and tyranny

Oya Affirmation

"I embrace the changes that flow into my life. I am open to transformation. I shift easily with all that comes to me. I am strong. I am capable. I am able to deal with anything that faces me. I have the ability to ride the waves in any seas."

Oya Associations

CRYSTALS	Fulgurite, septarian lightning stones, moldavite, meteorites
COLORS	Dark blue, dark purple, black, gray
PLANTS & OILS	Fern, cotton, rice, broom, alder, heather, thistle, saffron, bladderwrack, oak
ARCHETYPES	Shaper of Storms. Goddess of Weather. Fire Goddess.
SYMBOLS	Lightning, clouds, sword, storms, fire

"You have the power to cut through all things difficult or great in your life. Take this sword with you and know that the power is within you always to move forward on any road you choose."

Bring your attention back to your body, slowly open your eyes, and take a few deep breaths. As you step back into your day, take Oya's guidance and messages with you.

SUPERCHARGED MANIFESTATION

The goddess Oya is a powerful force who can shape the weather and change the flow of the Earth. She can help us to get energy moving where it is stuck as well as attract blessings, and she can aid us in manifesting our desires.

SUPPLIES

Rattle, tambourine, or drum (or noisemaker-making supplies, such as pie plates and dried beans or rice)
Natural offering (optional)

NOTE: If you do not have a rattle, you can use anything that makes noise. A drum, a tambourine, or even a makeshift drum such as a pot or pan would work. You can also fabricate a noisemaker by putting two items such as pie plates or cups together and filling them with a handful of dried beans or rice.

Decorate and embellish your noisemaker if you feel called. Go to a place where you will not be disturbed. You can do this ritual outside in bare feet to connect deeper with the earth or you can find a quiet place indoors. Root your feet firmly on the ground, take your noisemaker in your hand, shake it, and say:

"Goddess Oya, hear my plea.
From all stagnant energy, I want to be free.
Move away all obstacles from me.
As I will it, so shall it be.
I call my desires to me.
With each rattle, it shall be.
Shake, shake, for all the world to see.
All I manifest, now flows to me."

As you shake the noisemaker, feel the sound and energy. Sense it infusing your blood with movement, empowering your desires for change and manifestation. Envision it calling to the skies, to the storms, to the lighting and the thunder. Feel it calling to the goddess Oya. Feel the sound clearing away the blocks, the stuck parts of your life. Envision the rattling and the movement freeing the path forward so all that you want to manifest can flow.

If you are called to, dig deeper into the energy of the noise and allow your body to respond. If you feel inspired to dance, to stomp your feet, or to make vocal noise, allow what is unfolding. When you are finished, place both hands on the earth in reverence and in thanks to the goddess Oya for her aid, or leave her a natural offering.

RAIN SPELL: WASH AWAY THE PAIN

Oya is a powerful force of healing who can ease the pain and suffering that we offer to her. We can connect to her in nature when she comes to us in the form of rain. Do this practice during a rainy day.

SUPPLIES
A rainy day
Something natural to dissolve, such as Epsom or sea salt

Go outside in the rain somewhere you will not be disturbed and the salt will cause no harm to the Earth or animals. Place a little bit of salt in your hand, hold it up to the rain, and say:

"As the rains fall down, I am healed.
Washed clean, washed free.
All that was blocking me and holding me back
Is gone, dissolving into the earth.
Oya, bring me clearing and rebirth."

As the salt dissolves, envision all that is blocking you or that pains you being washed away.

BLESSING A BUSINESS

Oya brings blessings to those in business and was thought to be a protective force for marketplaces. This ritual can be done in any place of business, whether in the home or out in the world.

Crystals: Citrine, rutilated quartz, or green aventurine

Bowl in which to collect morning dew, rainwater, or snow

Full moon water (optional)

Salt

Place the crystals in the bowl. Leave the bowl on the grass overnight to collect some dew. You can also use rainwater or melted snow. If you only have a little, add what you can find to some full moon water. Take the crystals out of the water and add the salt.

Take the saltwater to your place of business and sprinkle some on the threshold. If it's an online business, carefully wipe a little on the back of the computer where it won't cause issue. Say:

> *"Goddess Oya, bless this place.*
> *Bring business flowing to this space.*
> *Bring me protection, bring me abundance.*
> *Bless me with wealth, opportunity, and growth, so it is."*

WEATHER SPELL: TO CLEAR THE AIR

The goddess Oya is connected to the weather and storms. We can connect with her to call these forces to sweep our lives clear of obstacles.

Open the windows in your house. You can also do this in your vehicle. The best time to do this is when there is a breeze, but anytime will do. Envision the goddess Oya, lady of storms, sweeping through your life, collecting the negative energy and cleaning it away. You can say:

> *"Goddess Oya, I call upon you to usher the winds of change into my world,*
> *Sweeping away all ill and negativity.*
> *I call upon your lightning bolts*
> *To supercharge the movement in my life,*
> *To remove obstacles, and to unblock pathways.*
> *I call upon you, shaper of storms, to aid me in shaping my path forward.*
> *Keep my path clear, so I may walk it safely."*

9

LILITH

THE REBEL

THE REBEL

WILD FEMININE

SEDUCTRESS

GODDESS OF SACRED SEX

SPIRIT OF WIND AND STORM

Lilith's legend extends far beyond the biblical interpretation of her as a demonic monster. Lilith was originally part of Sumerian myth as a fierce force of wind and storms connected to the goddess Inanna.

LILITH INVOCATION

"Lilith, like you I embrace my truth, no matter how uncomfortable it is for others to accept. It's okay to do what is right for me. I don't have to be nice at the cost of myself. My sexuality, my body, and my attention are mine to give. I freely choose my own path. I will not bow. I will not bend to the will of others. Lilith, grant me the strength to walk from all that no longer serves me. Give me your power so that I can rise."

A GREAT huluppu tree once stood on the banks of the Euphrates River. During a storm, it was washed away and found by the goddess Inanna, who planted and cared for it. When Inanna reached her full powers, a bed and a throne were to be made of the great tree, symbolic of her queenship and sexuality. However, three beings lived within her beloved sacred tree: a bird in the branches, a snake at the base, and Lilith, who wished to make the tree her home, in the trunk. Inanna beseeched the hero Gilgamesh to chase them away and he did, after which he created the bed and throne for her.

Lilith's existence predates her tales in the Bible and she was a much more important, ancient goddess than she is usually portrayed to be. Lilith is a symbol of feminine rebellion against the patriarchy. In her Hebrew and biblical incarnation, she was Adam's first wife, who refused to get beneath him to make love. She rejects the oppressive rules and leads her own sacred rebellion out of the garden, choosing to leave and live in exile rather than bondage.

In her depiction as the rebellious first wife of the biblical Adam she painted with the brush of original sinner. Disobedient, disrespectful, and wild, she refused to bow. And so, she was made into a monster, cursed to give birth each day to 100 demons, which were killed. Quite a punishment for saving no to a man.

Lilith is often connected with sexuality, passion, and lust. As so often occurs in patriarchal stories, she is portrayed as a demon for refusing to lay down her will in deference to the dominant rule of her husband.

Lilith symbolizes our journey from the known into the unknown. She is the embodiment of standing up for our body, our rights, and our freedom and of the willingness to leave to make our own path. Lilith is a survivor. She tells us we too can find great strength when the storms of life rage and we are swept from where we once found comfort. We have the power to rebuild our lives how we see fit, and deserves a home to call our own.

Through Lilith, we connect with our refusal to submit, to bow down and be ruled by another. Her story is the ultimate rebellion in the face of the patriarchy, and through her we tap into a vein of feminine power. The snake was sacred to her, a link to the medicine of the Earth and to our realm. She is often depicted as having wings and bird's feet and claws.

VISUALIZATION

CREATING OUR OWN SACRED GARDEN

Lilith shows us we don't have to stay anywhere that we are not comfortable. She tells us we have the power to build our own sacred space away from those who would restrict us.

Lie down in a safe, comfortable place and take a few deep, centering breaths. Close your eyes and relax your body.

You are in a lush landscape with trees and plants growing wildly around you. The birds sing in the trees and the sun shines brightly overhead, illuminating the leaves. As you walk through the green paradise, you come to the goddess Lilith. She smiles, motioning to the greenery around her.

"Welcome to my garden. As you may know, I left the Garden of Eden because I refused to submit to the will of another. I, Lilith, was demonized, like so many of us are, when we say no to the games of the patriarchal rule that would subjugate us. We are not here to be dominated and ruled! To hell with their garden! Let them keep it, and their rules with it. We are not here to bow and scrape."

"When we come back to our ancient power and see that we can create our own sacred garden anywhere we see fit, then no one holds sway over us. We do not need their shackles! We have no desire for their games! At times in your life, you will need to reclaim your freedom and leave situations that are threatening to swallow you, body and soul. Let no one tell you that you may not leave the garden. You have the power to create your sacred space anywhere, to put down roots where you wish and to take them up again when you go. Know this! Speak now of what you wish to move away from, of what has oppressed you for far too long."

Lilith motions to the earth below.

"Speak it here in this sacred place, letting your intention for transformation be like a seed to the earth below. Plant it deep and water it well with your every breath."

Matters Associated with Lilith

* Rebellion
* Honoring our truth
* Declining the demands of others
* Sacred sexuality
* Honoring our own sacred sexuality
* Standing up to the patriarchy
* Rebuilding our lives
* Finding our own home or sacred space
* Saying no
* Survival
* Starting Over

Lilith Affirmation

"No means no. I decide for myself and my body what is right. I will not lay down my needs for anyone. I honor my boundaries. I embrace my sacred sexuality. I am whole on my own. I release the need to people-please. I plant and tend my own sacred garden. I freely put my roots wherever I desire. I am a powerful creatrix. No one has the right to tread upon me."

Lilith Associations

CRYSTALS	Serpentine, garnet, ruby, black obsidian, carnelian, jet, malachite, snowflake obsidian, black tourmaline, black kyanite
COLORS	Black, red, green
PLANTS & OILS	Vines, plants with thorns, Tree of Life
ARCHETYPES	The Rebel, Wild Feminine, Seductress, Goddess of Sacred Sex, Spirit of Wind and Storm
SYMBOLS	Owl, snake, tree

Open your fingers and uncover a seed. Holding the seed, envision what you wish to transform. When you are ready, press it into the earth below, letting it go into the soil.

> *"Feed your intention on the path forward in every action and breath. What you have released will transform from what is no longer wanted into what will serve your highest self. Go now and take with you the knowledge of the great power that lives within you to manifest all things."*

Bring your attention back to your body, slowly open your eyes, and take a few deep breaths. As you step back into your day, take Lilith's guidance and messages with you.

HONORING SEXUALITY VOW

Lilith was painted as a demon for honoring her own sexuality. She not only refused to submit to Adam, but was said to be a passionate woman who delighted in carnal pleasures. For this she was made into a monster.

For many reasons from religious conditioning to societal beliefs, we can come to view our own sacred sexuality as something dirty that needs to be hidden. This is far from the truth. Your own unique expression of sexuality is part of who you are. We each have our own thread within us, and it is up to us to express it, in the way that aligns with the truth of our being. With this practice, we will create a vow or dedication with which to honor our own sexuality.

SUPPLIES
Paper and pen

Take some time to relax and come into your body. You may feel called to have a bath, light candles, or do some yoga—anything that connects you with the present and with yourself. When you feel comfortable, write down the ways you vow to honor your sacred sexuality. It can take some time to find the right words, as we have been shamed for thousands of years for the expression of our sexuality. But it may look something like this:

> *"I am not ashamed of the temple of my body. I celebrate my desire for pleasure and I honor my needs. I am a sacred vessel. I honor the body that brings me pleasure and joy."*

You can make it as specific or as general as you feel comfortable doing in this moment. This practice is not about pushing yourself in any way; it's about affirming that pleasure is not evil and celebrating your unique way of experiencing it.

REBELLION FROM SETTLING PRACTICE

Lilith was a rebel for refusing to bend to the will of another. She honored her truth and would not bow. We can connect to this powerful energy when we, too, need to rebel and honor our freedom.

SUPPLIES

Small piece of paper and pen
Shallow, freezer-proof dish; Water; Freezer

Envision the way or ways you want to stop settling in your life. Write down exactly what you wish to break free from. Tear up the paper into tiny pieces, place it in the dish, and cover it with a little water. Place the dish in the freezer and let the water freeze. When it is frozen, take it somewhere away from your home and say:

"I break free, I shatter the past.
I settle no more. Now move away fast.
Away from me go, darken no more,
My life is mine again. Hear my roar."

Roar to the heavens and smash the ice on the ground, envisioning breaking free from settling. As it cracks and melts, see the ties melting and the paper scattering to the four winds, taken away by Lilith and her fierce storms.

BOUNDARY SPELL

At times, we may allow our boundaries to become trespassed by those who are not respectful. This practice can help to secure those boundaries once more.

SUPPLIES

4 small pieces of black tourmaline

Bury the stones at four corners of your home or room, concealed from view. As you place them, say:

"To the north, I secure the boundary,
Taking back my space and honoring this place.
I bid thee farewell, all that is not meant to be here.
This northern boundary is now secure."

"To the east, I secure the boundary,
Taking back my space and honoring this place

I bid thee farewell, all that is not meant to be here.
This eastern boundary is now secure."

"To the south, I secure the boundary,
Taking back my space and honoring this place.
I bid thee farewell, all that is not meant to be here.
This southern boundary is now secure."

"To the west, I secure the boundary,
Taking back my space and honoring this place.
I bid thee farewell, all that is not meant to be here.
This western boundary is now secure."

Envision an energy boundary fusing through the stones, creating an energetic field of protection. After the ritual is done, ensure that you support your boundary by honoring your needs and saying no when you feel the need.

DARK MOON DETOX

The dark of the moon is a powerful time to go within, to detox, and to release. Just as Lilith released what no longer served her and walked away from the garden, we shed our skin during this time. This practice is best done the day before, during, and after the new moon.

NOTE: During a period of detoxing, we clarify the body to align and support our intention. Try to eat cleanly. Detoxing salt baths are can also release toxins from the body. Cleanse your home, clearing away clutter and using sacred smoke to clean the energy. This is also a powerful time for divination.

SUPPLIES
Black candle; Salt; Sage; Rosemary;
Black tourmaline, smoky quartz, or black onyx

Detoxing mantra:

"I release and let go of all that blocks my flow."

Surround the black candle with the salt, herbs, and crystal(s). Light the candle. Focus on the flame and envision the candle acting like a magnet, drawing the negative energy from you. As it flows into the candle, it is nullified and cleansed. Practice this during each dark moon before you do other rituals such as intention setting or divination.

10

MORRIGAN

THE PHANTOM QUEEN

GODDESS OF DEATH

LADY OF WAR

THE PHANTOM QUEEN

The goddess Morrigan is a powerful figure in Irish mythology. She's a fierce, battle-hardened sorceress imbued with the gift of prophecy and magick. Also called The Morrigan and the Phantom Queen, Morrigan had two sisters, Badb and Macha, with whom she formed a dark and powerful triad connected to the mysteries of death and destruction. The sisters often appeared near battles in the form of crows or ravens to carry the souls of the dead to the afterlife.

MORRIGAN INVOCATION

"Morrigan, I beseech thee, stand beside me in my battles. Give me the courage to make the choices that I need to make and the strength to act upon them. Give me your protection and your guidance as I walk forward. Gift me your sight so I may see the path ahead that serves me best. Oh, great goddess, guide me as I walk in the unknown."

MORRIGAN has been known to give out her dark prophecies to any who seek her wisdom. She foretold the fate of all. Her consort Dagda, or the Great God, sought her wise counsel and prophecy in the hours before going into great battles, eager to know the outcome, which she always gave to him.

She is connected to the dream realm and to that of nightmares, garnering both prophetic messages in dreamtime and in waking vision alike. She sees the truth in all things and can see all, even the end of all days.

The goddess Morrigan is a potent force for us to connect with when we wish to see things in a new light or tap into the unseen wisdom of the world. With her gift of prophecy, we can dive deeper into the messages we receive. She bids us to honor our intuition and follow the call of our inner compass.

Morrigan also teaches us of death and rebirth, the cycles of life, and to have courage in the face of the battles we fight. As sorceress, she tells us to honor our magick and to delve deeper into the rites and spells that call to us, for there is great power there.

As the phantom goddess, she can aid us when we need a little invisibility or shielding in our lives, offering us her dark cloak with which to drop deeper into the unseen.

VISUALIZATION

FINDING COURAGE ON THE BATTLEFIELDS OF LIFE

The Morrigan was a powerful figure during battles, lending her strength and prophecy to those going into war. We can draw courage from this great goddess during our own times of hardship and battle.

Lie down in a safe, comfortable place and take a few deep, centering breaths. Close your eyes and relax your body.

You are standing in a vast field, the horizon stretching in every direction. Dusk is settling on the world. In the distance, you can hear the cry of a raven coming into view. The large black bird perches on the ground below and transforms into the goddess Morrigan, long black hair falling down her back and dark eyes staring into yours, searching.

"I am The Morrigan, queen of the phantoms and sorceress of prophecy. You have found me on the battlefield, the war to come not yet begun. Many clamor for battle, not knowing the cost it will bring to them. I see these costs, though it is not my place to intervene. It is your choice which battles you fight. I am here to give you courage and strength, not judgment. Speak to me, now, what it is you wish to gather strength for in your life."

Take a moment to tell The Morrigan what you need courage for in your life.

"You have come here seeking strength for the road ahead, the path yet unknown to you. But I see it. I see the future of all things, the outcome of every choice."

The Morrigan holds her hands open and manifests a gilded cup filled with liquid.

"This brew is from my sacred cauldron. This is the broth that I imbue with courage, strength, and insight for those moving into battle. Will you take it now for your path ahead?"

Give your answer to The Morrigan. She offers you the cup. Drink deep and feel yourself getting stronger, more confident, and empowered to do the things you must do.

"Your path and the things you have spoken will be supported. You have the strength within you. You know the road to choose."

The Morrigan motions to the skies, where a conspiracy of ravens has begun to gather.

"My ravens whisper the secrets of the world to me. They know the hearts of all beings and all threads of fate, no matter how unseen. Many fear them and their dark powers. But they can bring boons as well as warning. They shall travel with you into your world and give you a touchstone of strength on your path ahead. They will be a guiding force of protection and will bring you messages. Travel well, my child, and believe in your power."

Matters Associated with Morrigan

* Death and rebirth
* Finding courage
* Protection
* Invisibility, shielding, and cloaking
* Truth, prophecy, and clarity
* Dealing with life's battles
* Triumph over enemies
* Dreams, visions, and nightmares
* Sexuality, love, and passion

Morrigan Affirmation

"I am courageous. I am strong. I am capable of handling all that comes my way. I weather all storms that enter my life. I am shielded from the self-serving intentions of others. I embrace the messages that flow to me. I open to my intuition and inner guidance. I honor the dark mysteries that flow within me."

Morrigan Associations

CRYSTALS	Bloodstone, ruby, black tourmaline, obsidian, red agate, garnet, black onyx
COLORS	Black, scarlet, red
PLANTS & OILS	Willow, juniper, aspen, honeysuckle, birch, oak, cherry, dragon's blood
ARCHETYPES	Goddess of Death. Lady of War. The Phantom Queen.
SYMBOLS	Raven, dog, wolf, horse, cow, sword, bow, bones, skulls, cauldron

Bring your attention back to your body, slowly open your eyes, and take a few deep breaths. As you step back into your day, take The Morrigan's guidance and messages with you.

PHANTOM QUEEN SHIELDING RITUAL

The Morrigan is known as the phantom queen, as she is the specter that spirits away the souls of the dead to the realm beyond the living. Because of this role, she is also associated with invisibility and shapeshifting, which shield her from the eyes of the living. She is the perfect force to connect with when we wish to move about more freely or to diminish our visibility. While this will not make you disappear entirely, it can help to make you less noticeable as you move about the world. You can do this when you need to be concealed.

Envision a large, dark cloak falling from your shoulders to the floor. The cloak has a large hood, one that is big enough to cover your head completely when it is flipped up. This is the robe of Morrigan, the phantom queen, which allows its wearer to be more unseen. Pull up the hood and envision yourself concealed completely within the folds of Morrigan's dark robe. As you do this, picture your energy field getting more compressed, bringing it toward the robe and into your body. Say:

"Dark lady, phantom queen,
Shield me, keep me unseen.
Protect me from all prying eyes.
Aid me with your dark disguise.
Keep all attention away from me.
As I will it, so shall it be."

DREAM/EVIL CATCHER

The Morrigan is connected deeply with dreams and nightmares, as she moves between the realms, and with the prophecy and messages that come through dreams. At times, less-than-pleasant dreams can plague us and the goddess Morrigan can help to protect us against these intrusive dreams.

SUPPLIES
Hoop, ring, or pliable branch
Black string
Decorations, such as beads or natural items sacred to The Morrigan (raven feathers, sticks, or dark stones and crystals)

If you are using a branch, carefully bend it into the shape of a hoop or tear. Tie the ends together to secure the hoop. Tie the string to the hoop. Moving clockwise, loop the string around the hoop every few inches. When you reach the spot where you began, thread the string into the loops. It should begin to look like a spider web.

Keep doing this, moving toward the center, keeping the string taut. Tie it off when you reach the center. Decorate it as desired. Secure a string to it so you can hang it.

Hang your dreamcatcher in a window near your bed. If you have no windows, place it near the bed. As you hang it, say:

"Goddess Morrigan, phantom queen,
Raven who dwells in the unseen,
Protect me while I take my rest.
Guard my dreams, keep them blessed.
Let no nightmare reach my ears.
Shield me from all ill and fears.
Goddess Morrigan, hear my plea,
As I will it, so shall it be."

STING AN ENEMY

Stinging nettles have long been used in folk practices as a source of protection against evil and dark forces. With this rite, we call upon the destructive energy of the goddess Morrigan to sever the ill intent of others toward us and for self-defense by sending a little sting to those who have wronged us intentionally.

SUPPLIES
Stinging nettle (wear gloves to handle)
Small candle
Knife
Small plate

A few days before you want to cast your rite, cut some nettle and place it somewhere to dry. Use gloves to handle it, as it will sting, and keep it out of reach of children and animals.

When you are ready, carve the name of the person you wish to sting into the candle and place it on the plate. Sprinkle the nettles around the candle and say:

"Meddle no more, settle no more,
Nettle, sting who would darken my door.
I now even the score, you know what for.
You shall bother me no more."

When the candle burns out, dispose of the puddle of cooled wax and the herbs far away from you. Dried stinging nettle can also be sprinkled anywhere that protection is desired, such as near homes, near doorways, or around the property.

RAVEN WING OF TRUTH PROPHECY

The Morrigan is a potent goddess to work with to connect us with the gift of prophecy. We can petition her at any time for clarity or help during divinations or for answers to the questions in our lives.

SUPPLIES
Black candle
Small piece of paper and a pencil
4 × 4 inch (10 cm × 10 cm) piece of black fabric, cotton or linen
Jasmine, Rose, Sage, Bay, Rosemary
Black obsidian
Black string

Gather all the items and light the candle. Take some time to concentrate on what you wish to know, and then write it down on the paper. Fold the paper toward you and place it in the center of the fabric along with the other items. Gather the corners together, secure them with string, and say:

"Phantom goddess, traveler between the worlds of spirit and flesh,
I gather this truth sachet for you to bless.
On your raven's dark wing, fly to me.
The truth of this inquiry for my eyes to see.
Oh Morrigan, gift me your prophecy,
As I will it, so shall it be."

Carry the sachet with you until you feel you have gained the answer you seek. You can also keep it by your bed or under your pillow for prophetic dreams and answers to your inquiry. When you have found the answer to your question, bury the herbs in the ground in thanks and offering to the goddess Morrigan for her help.

11

SPIDER WOMAN

THE WEAVER OF FATE

THE GREAT GODDESS

WEAVER OF FATE

WISE WOMAN

GREAT TEACHER

SPIDER GRANDMOTHER

Spider Woman is the Indigenous North American creatrix goddess of the universe, who spins the threads of destiny for all beings. As the great spinner of the fabric of life, she has many names, including the Weaver of Fate, the Great Teacher, Spider Grandmother, and the Great Goddess. She is also connected to the dream realm as the weaver of dreams. She weaves the fabric of fate, merging the known with the unseen. Her story of creation extends to many tribes.

SPIDER WOMAN INVOCATION

"Oh Spider Grandmother, she who spins and weaves the threads of fate, guide me to my destiny. Lead me to the pathway that is meant for me, and open me to the opportunities that it brings. Grant me your wisdom when I am lost and bless me with your guidance when needed. Help me to unravel the thread that is meant for me and help me to flourish on my path. I am open to the blessings of the universe."

SPIDER WOMAN is the embodiment of the earth and a goddess of protection for the natural world and her children. Together with the Sun God, she was the creatrix of the world and all beings who dwell in it. On her loom of fate, she weaves each soul a destiny to carry on their path into the living world. She has been called the Good Spirit among tribes and acted as their guide in all things. She taught the people how to spin and weave, thus creating blankets and clothing that would protect them against the deadly cold of winter and aiding their survival. It is believed that with her web of protection, she traps those who would do her followers harm.

Spider Grandmother brings us the medicine of honoring our path. She ties us to our destiny and our dreams and she reminds us that our fate is a thread we must unravel for ourselves. This can be a lonely prospect at times, but Spider Woman grants us the strength to move forward, knowing we can cut the threads that bind us.

Spider Grandmother offers warning to those who would imitate the path of another or try to steal their destiny. There are great costs for these offenses. She reminds us our greatest power lies in our own path, not in that of another.

VISUALIZATION

FOLLOWING THE THREAD OF DESTINY

Spider Woman weaves the threads of fate that encircle our lives. She can help us to unravel those threads and to embrace our path as we follow where it leads us.

Lie down in a safe, comfortable place and take a few deep, centering breaths. Close your eyes and relax your body.

Find yourself in a dark place. The world around you is cast in shadow. You hear a faint noise in front of you somewhere in the distance, and you move toward it. You enter the cave of the Spider Woman. The great goddess is seated at her loom, which hums as her thread slips through her fingers. Starlight shines from the thread and glimmers brightly from the spools spread around her in piles.

> *"Welcome, my child. You have found me working on my loom of fate. Here I weave the threads of destiny for each soul, guiding them on their journey from birth to death to being reborn once more in the stars. To honor one's path is to embrace the truth of all that they are. Here, upon my loom, I see each soul for the truth that resonates within."*

Grandmother Spider motions to the threads that lie in her lap and those that are woven in front of her.

> *"The tapestry of life is not always smooth. The threads can become tangled and frayed. Not everything is as simple as one would hope, but the thread remains there, a cord guiding you to your fate. Would you like to pick up your thread of fate and feel it with your own fingers? To connect with your path so that you may embrace it more easily in the living world?"*

Nod and take the thread offered to you by the goddess.

> *"Take this thread and follow it, now. It may show you the way forward or it may show you the past, but it is your journey. Allow that it may not be as you thought it would be."*

Pull the thread from the spool and move it through your fingers in a rhythmic pattern. As you move the thread, feel your deep connection to it, a resonance that flows through your being. Notice a sense of confidence that settles upon you as you know within your soul that you are on the right path. Impressions or images come into your mind, giving you insight or guidance into the unseen and the unknown. Take a few minutes to be here with the images that come to you.

The Weaver Goddess nods.

> *"You are well on your path, my child. As you continue forward, honor the truth of all that you are. Root yourself in your medicine and follow your happiness. The thread that is woven within you will always be there to guide you."*

Bring your attention back to your body, slowly open your eyes, and take a few deep breaths. As you step back into your day, take Spider Woman's guidance and messages with you.

Matters Associated with Spider Woman

* Destiny and fate
* Connection to ancient wisdom
* Manifesting the unseen
* Dream magic
* Cutting ties
* Weaving intentions
* Earth medicine
* Following our own fate

Spider Woman Affirmation

"I embrace my unique path. I move forward with ready steps toward the future that is meant for me. I untangle the mystery of my medicine and my purpose on this planet. I honor the truth that breathes within my soul."

Spider Woman Associations

CRYSTALS	Rutilated quartz, tourmalinated quartz, spider web jasper
COLORS	White, gray, silver
PLANTS & OILS	Reed, grasses, vines, ancient trees
ARCHETYPES	The Great Goddess. Weaver of Fate. Wise Woman. Great Teacher. Spider Grandmother.
SYMBOLS	Spider, thread, loom

CUTTING THREADS

When we need to cut ties that bind us, whether in relationships, jobs, situations, or wounds we need to release, this practice can help. It calls upon the weaver of fate, Spider Woman, to aid us in severing what we no longer need in our lives.

SUPPLIES
Candle
Two small pieces of light cardboard
One 18–24 inch (46–61 cm) piece of thread
Pen; Scissors
Fireproof container
Nettle; Rosemary

Gather items and light the candle. Tie the cardboard pieces to the string, one to each end. You can put a hole in each piece of cardboard if it makes it easier to tie. On one of the pieces of cardboard, write your name. On the other, write what or who you want to cut from your life. Place both in front of you, stretched out with the candle between them, and say:

"Though once we were tied,
The time has come to divide.
Oh Weaver Goddess, hear my plea.
Separate this [person/situation/issue] from me."

Pick up the scissors and the thread and cut the thread in the middle.

"I sever the past, cutting it fast.
Your time in my life has now passed.
Be gone from my sight.
So ends my plight.
Weaver Goddess, make it right."

Transfer the paper and thread to the fireproof container and set them alight. Add the herbs. When they have cooled, dispose of them away from your home.

DREAM ALTAR RITUAL

As Spider Woman is connected with the unseen, we can work with her to connect deeper with the mysteries of our dreams. This practice can help us to create a more conducive space for dreams and to invite clarity into the inquiries we have in dream time. Choose the herbs and stones that resonate with what you wish to create.

SUPPLIES

Sacred space, near your bed, on top of a small table or dresser

Chamomile for calm; Lavender for peace; Rose for prophecy; Amethyst for peace;

Purple fluorite for protection from nightmares; Moonstone for dreaming; Selenite
for peace

Collect your items and put them in a place near your bed or on your altar, where they won't be disturbed. You can collect all the herbs in a special bowl or shell. Place the crystals around your altar space. Dedicate this space to dreams:

> *"Lady of dreams, weaver goddess,*
> *This altar I make for you to bless.*
> *Grant me peace and dreams that are clear.*
> *Hold me safe and without fear.*
> *Gift me clarity and deep insight.*
> *Blessed be, Goddess, and now goodnight."*

If you have questions you wish answered in dream form, write them down and meditate on them before sleep. Leave the paper on your dream altar before bed.

WEAVING OUR FATE: INTENTION WEAVING

Intentions are powerful touchstones that connect us to our desires and what we wish to manifest in this world. The weaver goddess can help us with our manifestations and to weave our dreams into reality.

SUPPLIES

White candle

Three pieces of dowel or sticks, approximately 6 inches (15 cm) long

String; Herbs, crystals, feathers, or shells (optional); Pen (optional)

Gather the items and light the candle. Spend some time thinking of the intention you wish to weave. What is it you want to manifest into reality? Lay the sticks over one another, forming 6 equal ends in an asterisk shape. Tie the string in the middle to secure the sticks. Holding it tightly, weave the pieces together, going up and over alternating sticks on the way around, and say:

> *"With these threads, I do weave.*
> *My intentions, I open to receive.*
> *Manifest my need; help it take seed*
> *I believe, I receive. So it is."*

Keep your intention in mind and repeat the words until you are done weaving. Tie the end of the thread and make a loop for hanging. Decorate it as you are called with crystals, feathers, or shells. If you feel called to, write your intention on the hanging as well.

Hang your Intention Weaving somewhere you can see it each day and use it as a touchstone to support your desired manifestations with intentional action.

SPELL OF DESERVING

The Spider Goddess is the weaver of fate for each being on the planet. She is also connected with giving out what is deserved, good or bad. Eventually, we all get back what we give. We cannot outrun the goddess of fate.

SUPPLIES

Black candle
Item signifying the person you want to be dealt their fate. It can be a paper with the name on it or any totem you create to symbolize the person.
Black pepper

Melt the black candle, pour it onto the totem, and say:

"As this wax sticks to you,
  May your fate stick like glue,
  Holding all your words and deeds
  Planted deep within like seeds.
  May you reap what you have sown.
  Your earned fate you shall know."

Sprinkle the pepper onto the wax and envision the person's fate coming back to them, sticking to them like glue.

"My fate is not your fate.
  We now must separate.
  I bid thee farewell and end this spell
  And leave you to the Goddess Great."

Bury the cooled wax and totem somewhere far away from you or burn it in sacred fire to release it.

12

COATLICUE

EARTH MOTHER AND DEVOURER OF DARKNESS

EARTH MOTHER

SNAKE WOMAN

DEVOURER

GUARDIAN OF SOULS

Coatlicue is the Aztec earth goddess of life
and death, creation and destruction. She is depicted
as having the head of a snake and wearing a snake skirt
with a necklace of bones and human hearts. She is
the mother of all gods and mortals, and she held great
power in the ancient world. She has many forms; as
Tlazolteotl, she is the "eater of filth," and humans gave
up their sins and illness to her to be consumed.

COATLICUE INVOCATION

"Earth goddess of the sacred womb, snake goddess of birth and death. Within you all things are born and to you all things shall return. You are both cradle and grave to us all. Grant me the transformation that lives within you so I, too, can be reborn, renewed like the serpent to rise again from what I strip away. To you, I give all that ails me, and I am revitalized."

C OATLICUE is a goddess of creation and destruction, nourishing the birth of gods and mortals with her womb and giving them eternal rest within her body. She is the devourer of the dead, for the earth is where all bones rest and nourish the soil for what is to grow.

She is often depicted in the form of an old woman, symbolic of the ancient connection between the earth and the wisdom of the crone. Coatlicue is not the usual embodiment of mothering energy, which is often depicted as kind, caring, and compassionate. She holds the fiercer maternal energy of protection; she is said to be the goddess who watches over the souls that pass into the realm of spirit during childbirth.

As snake goddess, Coatlicue reminds us we are always shedding our skin, evolving, and growing into something new. We have the power to discard what no longer serves us to make the space for something new to grow, as we are always part of the cycle of death and rebirth.

In her incarnation as Tlazolteotl, she devoured evil acts and thoughts of humans and could absolve them of all wrongdoing. She took sickness and death from humans as well, purging them of the darkness that plagues them.

The goddess Coatlicue embodies creative energy and destruction, connecting us with the never-ending cycle of death and rebirth. She is a powerful goddess in her connection with the mysteries of the Earth. She reminds us of the power we can find in our connection with the natural world and the healing we can embody when we surrender to its mystery.

VISUALIZATION

TRANSFORMATION—SHEDDING SKIN

The goddess Coatlicue is a powerful ally and support during times of great transformation and change. By connecting with her, we can tap into the energy of the snake and the regeneration and guidance it brings.

Lie down in a safe, comfortable place and take a few deep, centering breaths. Close your eyes and relax your body.

You find yourself in a vast cave, cradled deep within the earth. The walls are high and there is a lot of space around you. Illuminating the clay-covered walls are torches, casting dancing shadows on the ground. In front of you, you see the snake-headed goddess Coatlicue.

"My child, there is great wisdom to be found in the womb of the earth. This is the place from which all things are born and where all things return when they die. We are one with this great planet, breathing in unison and moving through the ages. As the Earth prospers, so do we. The snake knows this. Each movement that it makes in its lifetime is in direct connection with the healing and wisdom of the earth below. It knows the mystery of the soil, each line of wisdom written on the sand. From this earthen guidance, it has learned how to shed its skin when it becomes too tight, casting off what no longer fits to make room for what shall grow."

The goddess lies on the ground and bids you to join her. Lay your body on the earth, feeling the supportive, grounding energy beneath you.

"We, too, hold the power of the ancient serpent within our bones. We have the ability to shed our skin and rise from the belly of the earth renewed. I ask you now, in this sacred earthen womb, to follow in the motions of the snake goddess before you and symbolically give up the skin that no longer fits you. Lay down what no longer has a place in your life so you may be transformed."

Take some time to think about what you wish to give up to the snake goddess. When you are ready, envision what you wish to shed falling away from you, from your body, from your heart. Let go of the relationships that hold you down, the beliefs that cause you harm, or the limiting thought patterns that keep you frozen. Picture them shedding from your life like snakeskin to the soil below, which absorbs it from your life.

"Shed the old to make room for the new. All things transform. Heal within the sacred womb and be reborn again. May the wisdom and blessings of the snake guide you on your path forward. May you never lose your connection with the Earth Mother."

Bring your attention back to your body, slowly open your eyes, and take a few deep breaths. As you step back into your day, take Coatlicue's guidance and messages with you.

Matters Associated with Coatlicue

* Transformation and shedding the old skin
* Connecting with the cycles of the Earth
* Offering illness or issues to be devoured
* Earth medicine
* Natural healing modalities
* Letting go of darkness or negativity that plagues us
* Death and Rebirth
* Mothers and Children

Coatlicue Affirmation

"I am connected to the Earth. I open to her healing and blessings. I shed what no longer fits me or my life. I am ready for new opportunities and growth. I honor the Earth and her medicine. I open to the blessings that flow toward me in every breath."

Coatlicue Associations

CRYSTALS	Serpentine, atlantisite, jade, fossils
COLORS	Green, brown, black, red
PLANTS & OILS	Cacao, "three sisters:" maize, beans, squash
ARCHETYPES	Earth Mother. Snake Woman. Devourer. Guardian of Souls.
SYMBOLS	Earth, snake, snakeskin, scallop shell

THE THREE SISTERS: OFFERINGS TO THE EARTH MOTHER

Agriculture was an important part of the Aztec world. The three most important crops were maize (corn), squash, and beans, which were sometimes collectively called "the three sisters" for the important interconnected roles they played as garden companions. The corn offers support for the beans to grow. The beans pull nitrogen from the air to benefit the plants. The squash shades the roots of the other crops. These plants were sacred to the Earth Mother, Coatlicue, who watched over the crops to help them thrive.

In her aspect of the Great Devourer, we bring to the goddess that which we wish taken from us, such as illness, negative thoughts, and old patterns. All can be released to the Earth Mother with this practice.

SUPPLIES

Candle
A small squash, top cut open
Small amount of dried corn or beans
Pen and paper

Place the candle, squash, and beans or corn on your altar. Light the candle and say:

"Oh great mother, I come to thee.
Hear this, your child's plea.
To you I give all negativity.
As I will it, so shall it be."

Write on the paper what you wish to be removed. Place it in the open squash and say:

"Oh great mother of death and life,
I give to you my stress and strife.
As it is taken, I shall give
These sacred offerings; reborn I shall live."

Take the squash outdoors to be offered back to the earth, symbolizing giving it to the Earth Mother. Bury it and the beans and corn in offering to her, visualizing what you wish to be removed from your life being devoured by the Earth Mother.

BANISHING SICKNESS: SPELL TO EASE PAIN

Coatlicue can devour all that is not wanted, including sickness. Use this spell with natural healing modalities as well as western or traditional methods to support health and wellness.

SUPPLIES
Potato

Potatoes have been connected with healing since ancient times, as they contain anti-inflammatory compounds and are absorbent. Cut the potato in half and rub its flesh on the afflicted area. Envision the potato soothing the affiliated area and absorbing the associated negative energy. Envision the potato getting darker as it fills with any illness or pain from the body and say:

"Goddess Coatlicue,
Great mother and devourer of disease,
To you I offer my distress
And ask for some ease.
I banish sickness and illness from my body.
I see myself as whole, all discord dissolved.
May what ails me be devoured by you, Great Mother.
May my body be healed."

Dispose of the potato far from yourself, preferably by burying it in the ground. Walk away from it and don't look back.

THE HEALING WOMB: SACRED BATH RITUAL

The goddess Coatlicue is the mother of all, and within her sacred womb all are born. We can connect with the energy of her infinite waters in this bath ritual.

SUPPLIES
Bath
Epsom salt
Essential oils (optional)

Draw the bath, consciously envisioning the pooling of healing waters, calling forward the presence and energy of the mother goddess Coatlicue. Submerge yourself in the waters and say:

"Oh great mother, I enter freely into your ancient waters,
  Your womb surrounding me and enfolding me,
  Giving me sacred space for rebirth.
  All waters are one, flowing from the same source.
  From you, I am healed, renewed, and rejuvenated.
  I am blessed. I am healthy. I am whole."

Take as much time as you desire to luxuriate in the sacred, healing waters, tapping into the connection of all water that runs through the planet.

DREAM PILLOW: TO DEVOUR BAD DREAMS

In her form as devourer, the goddess Coatlicue eats the darkness and filth that humans bring her. This dream pillow works in the same way, devouring the shadow that can influence our dreams.

SUPPLIES
Cotton batting
Fabric, any size
Needle and thread
Anise seeds, Bay leaf, Lavender, Chamomile

Gather all your items. Cut two pieces of fabric ½ inch (1.3 cm) larger than your desired pillow size on all sides. You can make the pillow large enough to sleep on if you feel called to, or you can create a smaller one that can be tucked under your regular pillow. Align the two pieces of fabric with right (outside) sides together. Stitch them together on three sides and turn the pillowcase so it is right side out. Stuff the pillow with the cotton and the herbs and, as you stitch the fourth side of the pillow closed, say:

"Goddess Coatlicue, devourer of all ill,
  Take away my nightmares, I've had my fill.
  Allow nothing to disturb my peace.
  Bless me with a good night's sleep."

Keep the pillow near you while you sleep.

13

IXCHEL

GODDESS OF THE MOON

MOON GODDESS

GODDESS OF DEATH

HEALER GODDESS

LADY RAINBOW

WEAVER GODDESS

Ixchel is the Mayan goddess of the moon and crone of death. She is said to be the mother of all the Maya deities, and she controls the cycles of the spirit from life to death. She is also connected with weaving, art, and music, and is a force of great inspiration for all those who seek her insight. She is often depicted as an ancient jaguar goddess and was also called Lady Rainbow.

IXCHEL INVOCATION

"Goddess Ixchel, lady of the rainbow and moonlight, guide my path forward, bathed in your wisdom and great insight. Show me how I can heal from the wounds of my past, and how I can walk away from unhealthy relationships. You are my light when times are darkest, and you heal my deepest wounds. I open to your great knowledge and the ancient wisdom of the moon."

IXCHEL is a goddess of medicine and midwifery. Her temple of worship is found on Isla Mujeres (Island of Women), which got its name from the sacred statues of the goddess and women that were on the island in tribute to her. The ruins of her temple still overlook the sea from the southern tip of the island.

The Lady of the Moon took the Sun as her lover, but he turned out to be a jealous partner. He was cruel to her, accused her of unfaithfulness with the Morning Star and kicked her out of his palace. Eventually he apologized and she returned, but the cycle repeated. One day, Ixchel had enough. She left for good, preferring to spend her time in the sky alone, away from the jealous gaze of her former lover the Sun. She claimed the night and traveled freely where the Sun could not go. As such, she became a protectress of women, of childbirth, and of the mysteries of women, guiding them and protecting them during their trials and triumphs.

Venerated as the creation goddess, Ixchel spun the fates of the souls on earth. She sat on her crescent-shaped throne and wove the stories of life on her great loom. Ixchel appeared in the guise of each of the triple goddess aspects—maiden, mother, and crone—to teach their wisdom to her followers.

Ixchel is a powerful ally when we look to connect to our own mystery and to ancient wisdom. She reminds us we don't have to put up with bad treatment from a lover and that we have the power to walk away and start again in a place where they will not bother us. Ixchel can help us weave a new life for ourselves, one rooted in our deepest truth. As moon goddess, she tells us to connect with the lunar cycles to manifest the life we want and helps to guide us in the unseen.

THE SACRED TEMPLE OF IXCHEL—GATHERING THE WISDOM OF THE GODDESS

In ancient times, people regarded Ixchel as a powerful connection to the moon and the heavens. She embodied cycles of time for the Mayans, and within her beams they gathered much wisdom. As lady of the rainbow and weaver of the cosmos, there wasn't anything that she didn't see or know. Ixchel can help us when we need illumination, guidance, and wisdom in our lives.

Lie down in a safe, comfortable place and take a few deep, centering breaths. Close your eyes and relax your body.

You are standing on a great rocky point overlooking the majesty of the sea. The blue-green waves lap at the edge of the rocks as daylight gives way to dusk. The moon rises on the horizon of the ocean, shimmering along the waves. Behind you is a temple, a large stone formation with an altar at its base. The moonlight illuminates the stones and within its beams the goddess Ixchel forms in front of you.

"Blessings, my child. Welcome to my temple on the holy island of Isla Mujeres. Here my followers came in ancient times to bring offerings to me, worshiping the old ways, cradled by the sea. Here they garnered my wisdom and blessings in the rays of the moonlight. Here they sought my guidance as I wove the rainbow threads of fate with the mystery of the moonbeams on my loom, crafting the cosmos and all things in it. Here in this sacred place, all is healed. All is known. All is transformed. Step forward toward my great altar and let the goddess of the moon aid you."

Step forward to the great stone altar. The goddess motions to its moonlit stones.

"Here on my altar, all truth is known. Hold out your hands and capture the wisdom of the moonlight. If it is healing that you wish, pour the moonlight where you want healing. If you desire clarity, think of what you wish for insight into and pour the moonlight on your brow and eyes."

Hold out your hands and capture the translucent moonlight in your cupped fingers. The light pools in your palms. Raise your hands and pour it over you.

"As the moonlight pours over you, all things are renewed. All is transformed by the goddess of the moon. If there are any troubles that you wish to leave behind, set them upon my sacred altar."

IXCHEL · GODDESS OF THE MOON

Matters Associated with Ixchel

* Lunar magic
* Offerings to the moon
* Cycles
* Feminine wisdom
* Healing
* Letting go of unhealthy relationships
* Pregnancy
* Mothers and Children

Ixchel Affirmation

"I let go of all unhealthy relationships that no longer serve my highest self. I am reborn into connections that are in alignment with the truth of all that I am. I connect with my darkness and my light. I am the master of my destiny. I am the weaver of my fate. I embrace the divine wisdom that flows in my veins."

Ixchel Associations

CRYSTALS	Selenite, moonstone
COLORS	White, silver
PLANTS & OILS	Moonflower, four o'clocks, night-blooming jasmine, wax plant
ARCHETYPES	Moon Goddess. Goddess of Death. Healer Goddess. Lady Rainbow. Weaver Goddess.
SYMBOLS	Moon, jaguar, dragonfly, rainbow, weaving, rabbit, spider, snake

If you have any fears, troubles, or issues you want to leave behind, place them on the altar. The goddess raises her hands in the moonlight and the issues dissolve.

"Take my magic with you into the world, knowing that I am in every moonbeam and rainbow to guide and help you. Fear not the unknown, for the truth of all things is just a moonbeam illumination away."

Bring your attention back to your body, slowly open your eyes, and take a few deep breaths. As you step back into your day, take Ixchel's guidance and messages with you.

MOON MAGIC: WORKING WITH THE CYCLES OF THE MOON

Each moon phase can give us powerful energy to work with for manifesting our desires and transforming our world. We can tap into the ancient lunar knowledge of the goddess Ixchel by following the cycles and lessons of the moon. Here are practices that we can do with each phase of the moon.

NEW MOON (DARK PHASE OF THE MOON)

New Moon Focus: Setting intentions and goals, focusing on dreams, and setting action steps. Renewal and rebirth. Nurturing, creation, dreaming.

Practice—Intention Setting: On the night of the new moon, write down your intentions for the upcoming month. Word them in such a way that they are already occurring, for example, "I am blessed with abundance" or "I easily find myself moving in the direction of my dreams." Write them out in a journal or offer them to the sacred fire.

WAXING MOON (NEW MOON TO FULL MOON)

Waxing Moon Focus: Increasing energy. Focusing on projects and ideas. Feeding intentions and goals with action. Gathering resources and implementing steps.

Practice—Feeding My Intentions: As we grow with the increase of the moon, we must feed our intentions. When we reach choices we need to make, we need to ask ourselves, "Is this feeding what I want? Are my intentions being honored by this? Is this supporting the path I want going forward?" Move toward what brings you closer to your desires in every breath and decision.

FULL MOON (BRIGHTEST PHASE OF THE MOON)

Full Moon Focus: Illumination, divination, clarity. Reconfiguring, adjusting steps or focus. Tapping into intuition. Celebrating what has already manifested. Charging items.

Full Moon Blessings: On the night of the full moon, light a white candle and say:

> *"Full moon clarity, all things I see. My desires I seed, Goddess bring what I need. Bless what has been and open to what shall be."*

WANING MOON (FULL MOON TO NEW MOON)

Waning Moon Focus: Decreasing energy. Rest. Release. Letting go. Releasing what isn't working. Giving thanks. Reflecting, dreaming, clarity.

Practice—Release: Pay attention to what isn't working with what you are trying to build so you can release or shift it. If they are mental blocks or thoughts you wish to get rid of, write them down and burn them in sacred fire. This is also a very good phase to clear away physical clutter in the environment that can be holding our energy back: Clean the home. Get rid of clutter. Let go of old relationships and patterns.

CREATING MOON WATER

Creating moon water is a simple practice done during the full moon. In it, water is left out to charge in the light of the moon, imbuing it with powerful lunar energy. Moon water can be further enhanced by adding a crystal or two to its waters.

SUPPLIES

Glass bowl

Water

Optional Crystals:
    rose quartz (love),
    citrine (abundance),
    amethyst (clarity),
    amazonite (healing)

Sealable container

Fill your bowl with cool, clean water. If using crystals, place them in the bowl. Find a place where it will not be disturbed but will sit overnight in the light of the full moon. Pick somewhere that the moon can reflect on its waters. If you can't, get it as close as possible. As you place your water, say:

"Lady of the moon, on this your brightest night,
Charge this water with your power and great insight,
Gift to me your illumination.
May all my intentions be met with creation.
Bless me with your sacred sight."

Let the moon water gather the energy of the moon overnight. Store it in a sealed container. Moon water can be used in many ways. You can add it to room sprays, herbal beauty products, bath water, or humidifiers, or you could use it for anointing.

If you use crystals to enhance your moon water with a specific vibration such as love or abundance, avoid ingesting the moon water, as crystal fragments can come off into the water and most crystals contain minerals that shouldn't be ingested.

DEALING WITH A JEALOUS PARTNER

The moon goddess had to deal with the anger of the Sun God when he unjustly turned his jealousy on her, stating that she was unfaithful to him. In the end, the moon goddess left him, preferring to choose her own path instead of suffering his abuse. Dealing with the jealousy of another can be difficult and sometimes the only way to break the cycle is to leave, just as Ixchel discovered. Before doing this practice, decide if you want to continue down this path with your partner or if you intend to sever the bond. This practice is aimed at releasing the relationship.

SUPPLIES
4 carnelian
4 bay leaves
Yellow rose
White or yellow candle
Fireproof container or contained fire

Gather the items in a quiet place. Write the name of the partner on the bay leaves. Arrange the carnelian and bay leaves around the candle. Light the candle and sprinkle the rose petals around it. Say:

"Even though I honor the past,
This jealousy cannot last.
Ixchel, give me courage
To turn the tide fast.
Away your jealous eye shall turn.
This relationship/negativity I now burn.
Go away from me; as I will it, so shall it be."

Burn the herbs and release the relationship. Support your intention by taking the physical space you need to end the relationship and end all communication.

BLESSING THE MOTHER (PREGNANCY BLESSING)

The goddess Ixchel is a protectress of women, children, and pregnancy. Her followers flocked to her temple and left offerings for blessings and protection during their time with child and afterwards.

SUPPLIES

Something to offer the goddess, such as flower petals or a natural item of your choice

On the night of the full moon, take your chosen offering outdoors. Place it where it won't be disturbed in offering to the goddess and say:

> *"Moon goddess, lady of the cosmic loom,*
> *I bid thee protect and bless my womb.*
> *Grant me your light, your strength, and your will,*
> *Keep us both safe. Give us your goodwill.*
> *Weave a strong thread of destiny for me and my child.*
> *May our days be sweet and our pain be mild.*
> *Oh great goddess of healing, protect us with your light.*
> *Grant me your blessings on this full moon night."*

14

BAST

GODDESS OF PROTECTION

· · · · · · · · · · · · · · · · · · ○ ● ○ · · · · · · · · · · · · · · · · · ·

GODDESS OF PROTECTION

WARRIOR OF RA

THE SACRED CAT

· · · · · · · · · · · · · · · · · · ○ ● ○ · · · · · · · · · · · · · · · · · ·

Bast (or Bastet) is a powerful Egyptian goddess connected with the wisdom of the moon, sacred anointing and perfume, cats, sunrise, and protecting women and children. She is often depicted as a fierce cat-headed goddess holding a sistrum rattle in one hand and an ankh, an Egyptian symbol of life, in the other hand. She is also known to appear in the form of a cat. She protects the house and home and ushers in prosperity. As she rules so many aspects, she can offer protection and abundance in all areas of life and so has been the patron goddess to many.

BAST INVOCATION

"Great Goddess of Cats, bless me with your power. Grant me agility to move through the obstacles in my life and the prowess to move about unseen by my enemies. Protect me with your Great Eye and allow me to maneuver safely away from danger. Usher prosperity into my life and bless me with your golden abundance. Anoint me with your favor, goddess Bast."

BAST is a warrior goddess and daughter of the great sun god Ra, who sent her to fight some of his greatest battles against his most ferocious enemies. Bast is also known as the protectress of Ra who keeps him safe on his travels through the sky in his blazing chariot. She is often connected to the goddess Sekhmet, her sister; together they were the fiercest protectresses of the pharaohs. She, like her sister, has also thought to be the all-seeing Eye of Ra. In ancient times, wearing a cat amulet was thought to be in devotion to her and garnered her protection and favor. Her followers also adorned their homes with statues of cats in her honor.

Like most goddesses, Bast has a dual nature: One side is connected with mothers and fertility. The other is associated with war and battle. Offerings were made to her for a healthy pregnancy, childbirth, and protection from illness and disease.

Bast brings the energy of fierce protection into our lives. This warrior goddess reminds us that we have the right to protect ourselves and that we need not stand down to anyone. She tells us to embody our fierce power and to roar when our boundaries are crossed. Bast tells us to stand up for what we believe and never settle for less than we deserve.

To connect with the watchful and protective energy of the goddess Bast and with the prosperity she brings, place a statue of her familiar, the cat, in a prominent location in your home. This way, the Eye of Ra can always be a fixture of protection.

SACRED SPACE SAFETY

Bast is connected with protection and guarding the hearth and home. In this visualization, we tap into that protective energy.

Lie down in a safe, comfortable place and take a few deep, centering breaths. Close your eyes and relax your body.

You find yourself in your home, sitting on the floor of your favorite room. You feel calm and at peace. In front of you, staring at you, is a large, dark cat with glowing gold eyes.

"I am the goddess Bast, and I have come to your sacred space today to offer you my protection. Once I had the face of a lioness, but over time I changed into the cat. Many said it was because I was domesticated, even though my powers as a goddess grew. People are so blind; they only see the obvious. I transformed into something that could move about unnoticed. What better way to protect my people and to be by their side than to take the form of a cat? So, as felines were invited into the home, I went with them, bringing my magic and protection with me."

Bast comes closer. Notice there is an ethereal glow in the room, a light surrounding all that you see. The light shield gets bigger. Watch as the wall of protective energy flows outside of the room and surrounds the whole building, which is now protected by the goddess Bast.

"I am a living shield, a cloak of protection to wear upon your shoulders. I will cast my guarding gaze upon you and your home. If ever you need me, you can call upon me and I will walk with you in this form to protect you. All you have to do is envision me seated by your door or home, casting my sacred light of protection upon all you desire."

Offer your thanks to the feline goddess. She dissolves into the light shield that surrounds your home.

Bring your attention back to your body, slowly open your eyes, and take a few deep breaths. As you step back into your day, take Bast's guidance and messages with you.

BAST · GODDESS OF PROTECTION

Matters Associated with Bast

* Protection of self, house, and home
* Honoring cats or familiars
* Security and safety
* Protection against malevolent spirits
* Promoting our wellbeing
* Drawing abundance
* Sexuality
* Pregnancy and child protection
* Tapping into our own magic
* Crafting potions

Bast Affirmation

"I am divinely protected. My sacred space is secure. I am safe. I am blessed with abundance. Prosperity flows to me in every breath. Opportunity is constantly coming to me. I am blessed by the universe. In every breath, miracles manifest in my life."

Bast Associations

CRYSTALS	Cat's eye, red tiger's eye, brown tiger's eye
COLORS	Gold, brown, red, white, orange, black
PLANTS & OILS	Catmint, catnip, valerian, vervain, cinnamon
ARCHETYPES	Goddess of Protection. Warrior of Ra. The Sacred Cat.
SYMBOLS	Cat, the sun, Eye of Ra.

CIRCLE OF PROTECTION RITUAL

As a protective goddess, Bast offers her defense to her followers. You can create this quick protection circle at any time or cast it before rituals or other spellwork to create some extra shielding during the sacred rites.

SUPPLIES
Black candle
Fireproof container
4 pieces of tiger's eye

Gather your items where you will not be disturbed. Place the candle in the center of the area in a fireproof container. Sit by the candle. Position the four stones around you, spaced equally. Envision a circle being formed by the stones, creating a protective barrier around you, and say:

"Goddess Bast, I call upon thee.
Protect me, Lady, wrap me in safety.
Guard me and shield me during this sacred rite.
Let me be safe, both day and night.
I am secure in this circle to work my will.
Grant me your powers so I have my fill.
Blessed be, Lady, for what you gift me.
As I will it, so shall it be."

This can be a good time to do other rites; for example, you could cast the protection circle before doing intentions on the new moon or blessings on the full moon. When you are finished, say:

"Thank you, great goddess, for hearing my call,
For this protective circle, which now may fall.
Let it dissolve from this sacred space,
But let safety come with me no matter the place.
Thank you, great goddess, for hearing my plea.
Blessed be."

PROTECTION POWDER

You can use this simple protection powder as an offering herb or sprinkle it outside the home, around the home or yard, or around the altar for some quick protection. Keep out of reach of children and pets. Substitute or omit any items you don't have on hand.

Mustard seed, Pepper, Salt, Sage, Rosemary, Thistle, Lavender, Mint
Bowl

As you gather the ingredients and combine them in a bowl, hold the intention of protection in your mind. Envision, with each herb or spice you add, a shield forming. Sprinkle the finished powder where you want protection and, as you do, envision a protective wall being summoned. You can also use the powder in small bowls around the home, out of reach of anyone. Use small jars or bottles with closed lids if they will be near children or pets.

FOUR CORNERS—SELF, HOME, AND PROPERTY PROTECTION

When you need to protect your home, yard, and property, this can be a good ritual to employ with the help of Bast. You can do this during the dark of the moon or on a Tuesday (Mars day) during the waning moon at sunset. Do this spell counterclockwise to banish negative energy.

SUPPLIES
Rosemary
½ cup (145 g) salt
Allspice, Clove, Sage, Star anise

Mix all the ingredients together. Beginning at the northern part of your yard, sprinkle a little of the mixture and say:

"Goddess Bast, hear my plea.
Protect all that is dear to me.
Guard me well; banish all ill.
So it is, it is my will."

Move counterclockwise (to the west next). Repeat the process at each direction point until you are back in the north. Then say:

"This spell is done, my will is cast.
Protect me now, secure it fast.
All ill away from [me/this place] goes.
Scattered away as the four winds blow."

You can also sprinkle some powder around doors or windows, making sure to keep it away from children, pets, or plants.

COPY RIGHT: RECLAIMING OUR WORDS

Others don't always have the best of intentions when it comes to what we create. Sometimes people would copy our words or try to steal our work. This is unacceptable to the goddess Bast, who protects her followers from harm and persecution.

SUPPLIES

Tape you can write on
Marker
Biodegradable balloon
Pin

Write the name of the offender who is stealing your work, truth, or voice on the tape. Blow up the balloon and place the tape on it. Hold the balloon, visualizing the party that has wronged you, and say:

"As you claim the words
From the mouths of others,
So too shall you be silenced.
The pain that you have caused,
You shall know.
As you have taken,
So shall be taken from you.
You are now muted, your power bound.
No further harm shall come from you.
I reclaim my voice; it is not yours.
As you have offended, the offense shall be revisited upon you tenfold.
So it is."

Pop the balloon with the pin and envision the power that this party had being obliterated. Hold the intention for their hold upon you to be broken and for karma to take care of their treachery. If it is a biodegradable balloon, bury it far away from you.

Make sure, in any case where someone is stealing your work, that you seek legal advice for protecting your creations.

15

PELE

GODDESS OF SACRED FIRE

FIRE GODDESS

MOTHER

GODDESS OF VOLCANOES

FIRE OF CREATION

Pele is the volcano and fire goddess of Hawaii, said to live within the volcano Kilauea on the Big Island. Known for her fiery temper, she is called "she who shapes the sacred land" because she devours and reshapes the terrain with the lava she expels. She is the embodiment of the island, with her body being the earth. She is known for taking the form of a beautiful young woman who can seduce anyone, but there are legends that paint her as an old woman who wanders the island in the company of a white dog—or sometimes in the form of the dog. Some who live on the island say they see her there to this day, most often in Kilauea National Park.

PELE INVOCATION

"Goddess Pele, your fire I invoke—your flow of ancient fury, death, and rebirth.
May my life be reborn, shaped anew, carved from the stones of the past. May
all obstacles in my path be melted away and flow from my life. May the flames
of creation spark illumination and inspiration in my world and flourish."

THE GODDESS PELE took many lovers, one of whom was the husband of her sister Na-maka-o-Kaha'i. She fled the anger of her sister, who came after her when she discovered their infidelity. Pele tried to create a new home away from Na-maka's wrath, but her sister flooded any land that Pele tried to create. Pele was finally successful in her creation of a home when she made a mountain that was great enough to withstand her sister's tirades, Mauna Loa.

Pele's emotion and anger could shake the Island of Hawaii to its foundations. She teaches us about the power we have at our core—power to move mountains with our fierce might and reshape the world as we see fit. She is connected to element of fire and calls to us to embrace the divine flame that burns within us.

Pele embodies destruction and rebirth, as she has the power to destroy the old and reshape the land into something new. When we connect to her great energy, we see how we can move mountains in our own world and create the landscape we desire.

REKINDLE OUR SACRED FIRE

Pele is a powerful force that connects us to our inner fire. We can work with her when we feel a disconnection between our inspiration and empowerment, rekindling our sacred fire.

Lie down in a safe, comfortable place and take a few deep, centering breaths. Close your eyes and relax your body.

You find yourself in a lush, tropical landscape on the side of a towering mountain. Vibrant green leaves surround you and the trees sway in the ocean breeze. Move up the mountain. As you walk, the lush green gives way to the crater of a volcano. You see the goddess Pele standing in front of you.

"Welcome to my blessed home, the sacred volcano Kilauea. I am Pele, lady of fire and passion. Here my power is made manifest, my fire shaping the landscape and fueling the transformation that surrounds it. So too, can we invoke elemental fire to shift the sands in our own lives.

For centuries, we have been taught that our fierce flame needs to be dimmed, our voices and desires rendered a whisper in the ever-growing sea of tyrannical rule. Our fury at the corruption of the world has been deemed insanity, downgraded from outrage to emotional tirades. But no more. The time has come to take back our power, to embrace the fire that burns within, and to live with the passion that we were born. Come, ignite the flame. Connect with the energy of my volcano, of the fire that burns deep inside the earth. Let it flow within you; let it empower your ancient wisdom to rise. See yourself as a flame, my child. No harm will come to you, but you will ignite your power."

You glow red like an ember, stoking the fire within. With each breath you burn brighter, feeling yourself tapping into empowerment. The flames rise higher. Feel any blocks within you melt away. When you are finished, the fire diminishes and is absorbed back into your body.

"Let all that no longer serves you burn away and let inspiration be born in its place. You carry within you the infinite spark of the universe. Let it guide you on your path forward. Know that your power is in your deepest truth; that is why they try to take it from you and silence it. Let your truth burst free."

Bring your attention back to your body, slowly open your eyes, and take a few deep breaths. As you step back into your day, take Pele's guidance and messages with you.

PELE · GODDESS OF SACRED FIRE

Matters Associated with Pele

* Releasing anger
* Elemental fire work
* Destruction magic
* Wanting to reshape your life
* Expression of emotion
* Embodiment of volatile feelings
* Creativity and inspiration
* Empowerment
* Manifestation

Pele Affirmation

"I embrace my inner fire.
I acknowledge my ability to reshape
my life. I transform the landscape
around me. I honor my fierce feelings.
I remove all obstacles from my path.
I can accomplish anything."

Pele Associations

CRYSTALS	Obsidian, lava rock , citrine, and carnelian
COLORS	Red, orange, black
PLANTS & OILS	Vines, moss, olive, fern, ti
ARCHETYPES	Fire Goddess. Mother. Goddess of Volcanoes. Fire of Creation.
SYMBOLS	Volcano, fire, white dog, lava

LAVA BEADS, BRING WHAT I NEED

As lava is sacred to the goddess Pele, we can tap into her ancient energy with lava beads. These igneous rock beads have a hard, sponge-like appearance. Their porous nature makes them popular for anointing with essential oils to carry the scent on a bracelet or pendant as we move about our day. You can add oils to intensify your intention, but they are optional. Pele has a superpower for making things happen. Here we can tap into her manifesting magic to aid us in attracting what we want into our lives. Practice this during the new moon, when we work with creating our intentions.

SUPPLIES
Elastic cord
Lava beads, any size
Essential oils, such as bergamot, cedar, orange, or peppermint (optional)

Gather the items. Decide on your intention and what you want to attract into your life. Keep your focus on your intention as you work. Cut the cord and string onto it the number of beads you've chosen. As you place each bead on the sting, say:

"Lava bead, bring what I need.
Pele, goddess of fire, bring forth my desire.
What I want will manifest; this sacred rite is blessed."

Tie the cord into a bracelet when you have reached the desired length. Envision what you desire coming into your life when you wear it. If you feel called, you can anoint your beads with essential oil to enhance manifestation and add the healing energy of the oils to the practice. You can use the beads as prayer beads as well, reciting an intention to Pele for each bead as you envision what you wish to manifest. You can repeat the mantra above as you pray upon each bead or you can say something specific, such as "I manifest soul-connected love into my life" or, "Abundance flows to me in every breath."

CALL TO ACTION

Pele is connected to primal action and in her action great transformation and movement take place. In this practice, we connect with her vital energy to invoke transformation and action in our own lives or to move things when they are stagnant.

SUPPLIES
2 or 3 carnelian stones
2 or 3 citrine stones

Orange peel, Lemon peel, Dried ginger
Red and/or orange candle
Pin

Gather the items. Place the stones, peel, and ginger around the candle. Using the pin, carve into the candle what action you want taken or what you need moved in your life. If there is a block preventing you from moving forward, for example, write how you want it removed. Light the candle, sprinkle a little ginger on the flame, and say:

"Elemental flame, I summon thee.
Action is sparked; my will shall be.
Where I need movement, things will shake.
It will move forward; blocks shall break.
Goddess Pele, your fire burns within me.
Action is taken; my will shall be."

To further invoke the fierce energy of Pele, stomp on the ground and raise the energy in the surrounding area, just as Pele shakes the ground. Envision all blocks being shattered and the path for action now being clear in front of you.

SACRED FIRE: RELEASING TO THE FLAME

Pele embodies elemental fire in her connection to volcanoes and lava. We can connect with her purifying energy in the form of a fire release, which is a simple offering that involves letting go of what we no longer wish to have in our lives to the sacred flame.

SUPPLIES
Fire
Paper and pencil

This is best done outdoors or using a fireproof enclosure or container. Build a fire. Write down on the paper what you wish to release. It can be old habits, beliefs, situations, or people—anything you want cleared from your life. Offer the paper to the fire and say:

"Fire burning, oh so bright,
Illuminate all with sacred light.
Take from me what I release.
In its place, gift me peace.

To the flames I let this go.
From my life it now flows.
Goddess Pele, take from me
What I don't want, so I am free."

Envision what you want released leaving your life for good as it is consumed by the flames.

RESHAPING RITUAL: CARVING OUR DESIRES

Pele continuously reshapes the landscape that surrounds her on the Island of Hawaii. We can tap into this potent energy of transformation and reshape the foundations of our own lives. We can also create a vision board to support our desires and connect us further to our manifestation.

SUPPLIES

Red candle
Block or piece of air-dry clay
Something with which to carve the clay
Items, such as crystals or other natural things (optional)
Cardboard and images of what you desire (optional)

Gather the items and light the candle. Envision what you want to bring into your world. Shape the clay into a representation of your intention. You can either form it into a totem or object of your desire or into a disk marked with symbols, creating a sigil representing what you want to attract into your life. There is no wrong way to create your desire. As you create it, envision the life you wish to embody or picture what you want as part of your life.

"Goddess Pele, as you reshape the land, so I reshape my life. I carve my desires
with my own hands. I see all things as possible and I know that I have the power
to create anything that I wish. My world is mine to build. So it is."

You can add other items to your desire, such as crystals or other natural things, to decorate it and further enhance your manifestation. Allow the clay to dry. Keep it where you can see it each day as a touchstone of your intention.

If you feel called to, you can further intensify the manifestation power by creating a vision board of your intentions. Find images or phrases that embody your desire and affix them to a piece of paper or board. Place the vision board on your wall where you can see it each day.

16

CERRIDWEN

PRIESTESS OF THE CAULDRON
AND GODDESS OF AVALON

- ● ● ● -

GODDESS OF AVALON

LADY OF THE MOON

PRIESTESS OF THE GREAT CAULDRON

THE WHITE LADY

- ● ● ● -

Cerridwen is a powerful Welsh goddess of
knowledge, magic, and transformation. She is one of
the five goddesses connected with the sacred Isle
of Avalon and she is the keeper of the sacred cauldron
of death and rebirth, in which she brews her magical
potions and spells. She also symbolizes inspiration,
taking the path unseen, and opening to a new road
we may not have considered.

CERRIDWEN INVOCATION

"Great Goddess of the Cauldron, priestess of the Isle of Avalon, grant me your wisdom and insight into all things. Within your sacred waters, may I come to know the truth of all things. May I flow freely with the cycles of death and rebirth that move through my life. May I connect with the great knowing of the universe and the ancient ways that sing in the skies."

CERRIDWEN is usually portrayed in the crone aspect, but she also represents the goddess triad—maiden, mother, and crone—herself. As she is connected with the moon, she is a prophetic goddess who can tell the fate of all beings. In her aspect of creative and poetic goddess, she is the White Lady of inspiration and death, her cauldron containing the essence of divine inspiration.

In one tale of Cerridwen, she was the mother to the greatest of all bards. It was said that she had a son who wasn't handsome, so she sought to create a potion to make him wise. For a year and a day, she toiled on the potion. When it was nearly complete, three drops fell onto her serving boy, and he was changed into a powerful magician. He fled from the angry Cerridwen. The pair transformed into various animal forms during their chase—a hound hunting a hare, for example, and an otter pursuing a salmon. Finally, he turned himself into a kernel of grain. She turned herself into a hen and ate him. She became pregnant, and in nine months Taliesin was born. He became known as the Chief of Bards and was connected to King Arthur and the Knights of the Round Table. He inherited the gift of prophecy from his mother and could see into the future, as well as her wisdom surrounding potions and healing.

Cerridwen is best known for her magick and the spells she crafts in her cauldron. Within its confines, she can create anything, blessing or curse. She is considered the lady of transformation on Avalon. In her cauldron, the great mysteries of the universe are revealed; she knows all things and can influence them.

Cerridwen teaches us transformation and inspires us to embrace the change that surrounds us, moving with the natural patterns of death and rebirth that flow through our lives. Each ending is but a beginning. In her guise as moon goddess, she shows us the power to make magick with lunar energy and whispers the ancient ways to the ready ear of the witch. Cerridwen whispers inspiration to us and tells us to embrace the wisdom flowing in our veins so we can live our deepest truth and calling.

THE CAULDRON OF CERRIDWEN

The Great Cauldron of Cerridwen is a powerful gateway to magick, transformation, and rebirth. Within it is revealed great wisdom and mystery.

Lie down in a safe, comfortable place and take a few deep, centering breaths. Close your eyes and relax your body.

You find yourself on the shores of a beautiful island, the green trees swaying in the breeze. The crystalline waters that lick the shoreline seem to hum with magickal energy. The moon, a perfect crescent pendant in the darkness, hangs high in the sky. Walk up the hillside toward a clearing where a silver-haired woman stirs a great cauldron.

"My child, welcome. I am Cerridwen, one of the ancient priestesses of this island of Avalon. Here within the sacred veil, all mysteries are known, for this is the birthplace of magick."

She motions to the great lake that glimmers in the distance.

"Beyond the horizon, a mist gathers around this ancient isle, protecting it from eyes that do not have the sight to see her great mystery. My great cauldron is the source of these mists filled with the waters of Avalon; they rise from my magick and protect this land. You are here because the ways are known to you, written on the marrow of your bones. You have come here seeking the guidance of the great cauldron, insight into the unseen."

Cerridwen motions for you to approach the cauldron. Move beside it and stare into its depths.

"The cauldron is different things to different beings, and each one of us gleans a unique medicine from these waters. Come, stare into the depths. Seek the wisdom of what has brought you here. Do you desire answers? Clarity? Inspiration? Within the sacred waters, all things are possible. Ask the cauldron and take the waters unto yourself."

Stare into the cauldron, which reflects back to you the moonlight overhead, your reflection, and Cerridwen at your side. The water changes and you see images float across the surface, flowing from one into the next—a series of symbols and shapes that answer your inquiry. Take a few moments to allow the messages to flow to you. Cerridwen motions for you to scoop some of the water into your hand and drink. Follow her lead.

Matters Associated with Cerridwen

* Ancient wisdom and knowledge
* Honoring ancestors and the dead
* Sacred rites
* Shamanic practices
* Hexes
* Divination and prophecy
* Transformation
* Poetry
* Crone medicine

Cerridwen Affirmation

"I connect to my creative energy. I am inspired by my desires. I follow the direction of my heart. I honor my intuition and follow my inner compass. I am connected to the magic that flows within my soul."

Cerridwen Associations

CRYSTALS	Moonstone, selenite, labradorite, black tourmaline
COLORS	White, black
PLANTS & OILS	Willow, vervain, birch, rowan, oak
ARCHETYPES	Goddess of Avalon. Lady of the Moon. Priestess of the Great Cauldron. The White Lady.
SYMBOLS	White sow, cauldron, cattle, dog, hawk, cat, grain, crescent moon

"The mystery of the cauldron is known only to a few, and you have tasted of her waters. They hold the magic of Avalon, the insight into all things. Take this knowledge with you when you go, and follow the inspiration that it brings, as it will flow into all aspects of your world."

Bring your attention back to your body, slowly open your eyes, and take a few deep breaths. As you step back into your day, take Cerridwen's guidance and messages with you.

HONORING ANCESTORS

The goddess Cerridwen honors the cycles of life within her sacred cauldron, stirring the tides of death and rebirth. In her ancient wisdom, she is connected to the ancestors and their great knowledge. With this ritual, we honor those who have gone before us into the spirit realm.

SUPPLIES
Photos and mementos of loved ones
Candles (optional)
Offerings of food and drink

Set up a sacred place to display photos of your loved ones and sacred items of remembrance. Add candles, if you feel called to, or anything that you feel honors your loved ones. If you wish, you can say something, such as:

"Always with me, never forgotten,
The thread of memory that binds us sweet;
You shall be remembered, you shall be honored
Until the next time we are able to meet."

When you are finished, leave offerings of food and drink and have some yourself in celebration and remembrance of those who have ventured ahead into the spirit realm.

INSPIRATION RITUAL

Those who seek inspiration often go to Cerridwen to gain her insight and clarity. This practice can help to inspire us to say the right words, follow a new path, or try new things.

SUPPLIES

White candle
Bowl
Fresh water
Rosemary, Lemon peel
Symbolic supplies (if specific; see directions)
Peppermint or lemon tea
Natural linen cloth
Jar with lid

Gather the items and light the candle. Pour the water in the bowl and add rosemary and lemon peel. Say:

"In Cerridwen's great cauldron, inspiration does brew.
Oh White Lady, bless me true.
Ignite the sacred fire that burns within me
With imagination, illumination, and creativity.
Remove all blocks that stand in the way.
Priestess of Avalon, inspire me this day."

Strain the herbs and peel from the water using the cloth and jar. If you looking for inspiration for a specific type of creation, such as art, gardening, or writing, add your art supplies, trowel, or pen and paper, for example, around the candle.

Use the water to anoint your items and imbue them with inspiration. If you are looking for general inspiration, anoint your brow and third eye with the water. Say:

"By leaf and peel, inspiration is revealed.
Flow through me, goddess of creativity.
All things I see; the path is revealed to me."

Make some tea for yourself and relax. Take some time to allow inspiration to flow. Thank the goddess for her inspiration and insight.

CERRIDWEN'S HEX

When a banishing or binding isn't enough, you may need to employ a hex on someone who wishes you great harm. Hexes are powerful and not to be used lightly. But, when others come at us with harm in their minds or hearts, sometimes hexes are the only way to be rid of them.

SUPPLIES
Black candle
Pins

Carve the name of the person you want to hex onto the candle. Light the candle. As it burns, stick a pin in it and say:

"With pin one, your action is done.
No more shall you cause me ill.
Your intentions are at an end.
No more evil will you send.
By pin one, your actions are done."

Stick a second pin into the wax.

"With pin two, your actions are through.
No more shall you wish me spite.
Your curse is now weak.
Of me you shall no longer speak.
By pin two, your actions are through."

And finally, stick pin three into the wax.

"With pin three, you forget about me
And away from me you go.
Your evil is gone forever.
You will think of me never.
Or by pin three, Cerridwen's punishment you shall know."

Let the candle burn down. Envision being protected from the person's energy and that, as the wax melts into a pile, so does their power. Once the candle burns out, let the wax cool. Bury the wax and pins somewhere far away from you.

HALT GOSSIP

If you are the victim of gossip and other methods have failed to stop it, you can ask for help from the goddess Cerridwen.

SUPPLIES
Candle
Paper and pen
Scissors
Tape
Cloves
Fireproof container

Gather your items and light the candle. On the paper, draw the figure of a person. It doesn't have to be exact; it can be in the shape of a gingerbread person. Give the little figure eyes, a nose, and a mouth. Cut out the figure. With the pen, write the name of the gossiper on it. Cover the figure's mouth with a piece of tape and say:

> *"This gossip now stops; your lips are now sealed.*
> *Against you I now place a shield.*
> *You will stop speaking against me, in all shape and form,*
> *And if you do not you incite Cerridwen's dark storm."*

Light the paper and let it burn in the container.

> *"As this paper does burns, so the gossiping does end.*
> *Away now your attentions I do send.*
> *Leave me be, go away,*
> *Or Cerridwen's price you will have to pay."*

17

SEKHMET

GODDESS OF FIRE, DESTRUCTION, AND JUDGMENT

THE DESTROYER

JUDGE OF HUMANKIND

PUNISHER OF RA

EYE OF RA

SCARLET LADY

GODDESS OF THE SUN

Sekhmet is the retribution goddess of Egypt. She is often called the Eye of Ra and depicted with the head of a lioness and holding an ankh, the symbol of life. She is known as a powerful warrior and fire goddess. It is said that when the Egyptian god Ra was angry with mankind and in his frustration ripped out his own eye and threw it at them, it became the Goddess of Judgment, Sekhmet. She passes the sentences Ra hands out to humankind. She is the eye that sees all; nothing escapes her sight. In this way, she can judge all beings, as she knows all things.

SEKHMET INVOCATION

"Goddess Sekhmet, lady of retribution and judgment, hear me. I invoke your wrath, your fire, so that I may defend myself. May you intercede on my behalf with those who have wronged me, your vengeance swift and just. Hear me, oh great lioness of fury, protectress of your followers, and warrioress of light. Protect me. Guard me. Avenge me."

SEKHMET represents a fierce aspect of the feminine, a fiery and sometimes destructive force. She is a protectress of women, defending them with her righteous anger and coming to their aid when balance is needed. She is a double-edged sword, connected to both warfare and healing, a power of creation and destruction. Known as the Scarlet or Red Lady, she led the pharaohs in warfare and hungered for blood. She was also said to have punished those who wronged her, with pestilence and disease.

As she was such a force to be reckoned with, sacrifices often have been made in her honor to appease her ferocious hunger for destruction. In her aspect as healer goddess, she teaches medicinal healing and is a patron goddess of healers. As the goddess of the sun, she has a glowing red disk upon her head held in place by a cobra. In this aspect, she is connected with the energy of fire, heat, and destruction as she embodies the desert sun and its scorching flame.

Sekhmet shows us there are times where we must stand up for ourselves with anger and fierce conviction. She tells us that sometimes we need to destroy to create, embracing our fire; sometimes the past needs to be burned to be renewed. Sekhmet helps us to obtain justice for wrongs and breathes protection around us when we need it most.

WISDOM OF SEKHMET

The goddess Sekhmet is a powerful ally for gaining deeper insight. As the Eye of Ra, she sees all; nothing is hidden from her gaze. We can connect with her when we wish to gain deeper insight and wisdom.

Lie down in a safe, comfortable place and take a few deep, centering breaths. Close your eyes and relax your body.

You find yourself in the middle of a vast desert, the bright sun shining down on you. Walk forward on the hot sand toward a small, palm-lined oasis in front of you. Enter the oasis. You are met by the goddess Sekhmet. She is tall and stately with the head of a lioness, wearing the sun as a disk on her crown.

"Welcome to my desert oasis. I am Sekhmet, goddess of the sun, warrioress of destruction, and all-seeing Eye of Ra. I am the embodiment of vengeance and retribution for the ills caused to my followers. I show those loyal to me how to defend themselves from those who would do them harm. Have you come seeking my insight and wisdom?"

Nod your head.

"Then my guidance you shall have. Speak now to me all that you wish clarity on. Tell me your fears and your doubts. Speak now to the Goddess."

Take some time and tell the goddess Sekhmet what you wish clarified in your life. She nods her lioness head and motions to the sun disc she wears.

"I am the light of illumination; nothing is hidden from my sight. Hear me now, for I will give you the answers that you seek."

Take some time and listen to what Sekhmet says to you. Open yourself to the messages that flow from her all-seeing wisdom and insight.

"Take my wisdom back with you, away from the desert and into your life. Pay heed, for more messages may unfold for you. Be aware, for my eye is everywhere."

Bring your attention back to your body, slowly open your eyes, and take a few deep breaths. As you step back into your day, take Sekhmet's guidance and messages with you.

SEKHMET · GODDESS OF FIRE, DESTRUCTION, AND JUDGMENT

Matters Associated with Sekhmet

* Destruction
* Channeling righteous anger
* Awakening
* Protection of women and childbearing
* Judgment or legal matters
* Action

Sekhmet Affirmation

"I embrace my fire. I open to my fury. I acknowledge the anger flowing within me. I take action on those who would do me wrong. I know that I am worthy of divine justice. I am protected. I am safe."

Sekhmet Associations

CRYSTALS	Tiger's eye, cat's eye, leopard skin jasper (jaguar stone), topaz, sunstone
COLORS	Black, red, gold, yellow
PLANTS & OILS	Catnip, frankincense, myrrh, heliotrope
ARCHETYPES	The Destroyer. Judge of Humankind. Punisher of Ra. Eye of Ra. Scarlet Lady. Goddess of the Sun.
SYMBOLS	Lion, Eye of Ra, cat, cobra

DESTRUCTION RITUAL: MOVING ON FROM THE RUBBLE

Try this ritual when you wish to move on from what no longer serves you or your highest good. When the time comes to move on from the rubble of the past that has crumbled behind us, Sekhmet can be a good ally.

Choose something that embodies what you wish to move away from. If it is an old relationship, for example, maybe you have a photo or old article of clothing belonging to the person you wish to move on from. If it is a job, maybe you have a paystub. If it is a place you live, maybe you have a rent receipt. Choose something that represents the connection.

SUPPLIES
Something to symbolize what you wish to move away from
Scissors (optional)

Destroy the symbolic item with scissors and/or your hands. Shred it and say:

"I move on from the chaos and open to the new.
I destroy what was and what it put me through.
I release the past I no longer need.
Never again will it make me bleed.
Goodbye and farewell; that path is no longer for me.
As I will it, so shall it be."

Discard whatever remains in an appropriate manner that gets it far away from you. Bid farewell to the past and walk away. Feed your intentions to move on from the past by supporting your goal with your choices: Look for a new job or a new home. Set boundaries. Make the decisions that feed your intentions.

BURN A CURSE: RELEASING A CURSE

At times, we may feel we are the victim of a curse or ill wishes of another. The goddess Sekhmet, lady of vengeance and retribution, can aid us in releasing this energy and thwarting the curse.

SUPPLIES
Black candle
Paper and pen
Pin
Shovel
Fireproof container

Gather your items and light the candle. Write down who or what you believe has cursed you, and then fold the paper away from you and seal it with some drips of wax. With the pin, carve the Eye of Ra or other eye symbol onto the wax seal and say:

"I bind this curse. It will do no worse; reverse, reverse. I release this curse.
All harm will disperse, as I speak this verse; reverse, reverse. I release this curse."

Take the paper to a place, preferably not on your own property, where you can safely and legally burn and bury it. Dig a grave to bury the curse, burn the paper in the container, and say:

"Goddess Sekhmet, all-seeing Eye,
Dispose of this curse; no more will they try.
Their will is dissolved, their efforts for naught.
This curse now is dead; in the ground it shall rot."

Once the paper is burned and only ash remains, drop them into the hole and bury them. Say farewell to your curse and walk away, never looking back.

FAVORABLE JUDGMENT PETITION

As the Eye of Ra, the goddess Sekhmet carries out sentencing and retribution on those she holds in judgment. She is a powerful goddess to connect to when we are in legal battles or face judgments that could use some of her power. Petitioning the goddess is as simple as specifying to her what aid you need. It can be as easy or complex as you desire to ask her for favorable judgment.

SUPPLIES
Pen and paper, if desired
Offering

For this practice, speak the truth of your heart. Identify where you need favorable judgment, and speak it to the goddess Sekhmet. For example:

"Goddess Sekhmet, hear my plea.
Give favorable judgment in ____ to me.
My cause is just, my heart is pure.
Help me now to make judgment sure."

Hold the vision of the outcome that you desire. Give thanks to the goddess for her help and leave her an offering.

SUCCESS RITUAL

Sekhmet is connected with the sun and fire energy. She is a deity of action, of getting things done and moving things forward. We can tap into this energy when we seek success.

SUPPLIES
6 sunstones
Red, orange, or yellow candle
Pin

Arrange the sunstones equally spaced around the candle, forming a sun shape. Carve the candle with a sun sigil. Light the candle. Envision the success you want. This can be in a business, a specific situation, or anywhere you need success. Say:

"Burning bright, my desires ignite.
What I wish for is within my sight.
Success for me, for I am blessed,
Fire and sun, my will be done.
Goddess Sekhmet, lady of the flame,
Bring success to my name.
What I wish for comes to me.
As I will it, so shall it be."

Carry the sunstones with you as a touchstone for your intention or keep them in a place where you can see them often, such as by your bed or upon a sacred altar.

18

DURGA

WARRIOR GODDESS OF STRENGTH

· ● ● ·

WARRIOR GODDESS
PROTECTIVE MOTHER
GODDESS OF STRENGTH

· ● ● ·

Durga is a powerful protection goddess in India. She is usually depicted riding a fierce tiger and having ten to eighteen arms. Within her grasp are items that represent defense and protection, such as swords, bows, shields, and staffs, as well as sacred ritual items for her ancient rites. With her vast power, she is the destroyer of evil that would plague humankind. She is a fierce protectress, and all tremble in the shadow of her might. Her name means "inaccessible" and "impassable" in Sanskrit, as she is invincible. Durga is the embodiment of fierce mother energy, shielding her children from harm.

DURGA INVOCATION

"Goddess Durga, fierce mother and protectress of all of your children, empower me and give me courage on my path ahead as I step into my power and deepest truth. Guide me and keep my path clear of blocks, cutting away all obstacles with your sacred sword. I know my strength, and I will not back down from the challenges that face me. I too will stand, sword in hand, and never back down."

D URGA was created by the gods to destroy a buffalo demon no one else could vanquish. Even the strongest gods were no match for it, but Durga destroyed it. She can also be called upon to get rid of unwanted internal forces such as jealousy or negativity.

Known as warrior goddess of strength, she is also called Durga Maa (mother). She is connected with death and rebirth in her roles as destroyer and protective mother.

Durga is also connected with truth. She calls us to root ourselves deeply in all aspects of our authenticity. As the slayer of demons, she reminds us we need to be present and in the moment to fight the battles that rage, to face our fears, and to have courage even in the face of the unknown.

On her fierce tiger, Durga bids us to take back our power and our voice. The time has come to rise up and roar, she reminds us. She brings us strength when we feel powerless. She is an avatar of fierce feminine energy, telling us to never give up and that there is always a way to defeat and transcend what blocks us on the path forward. She is the perfect goddess to work with when we need motherly protection from the world while we set out to live our deepest truth. Durga wants us to answer the call to lead, to rise up and follow our deepest truth.

Navaratri, meaning nine nights, is a festival that celebrates Shakti, or sacred energy of the divine feminine. The nine forms of the goddess Durga are worshiped during Navaratri, which is also called *Durga Puja*.

RIDING THE TIGER

Durga is a powerful force to connect with when you are facing obstacles and need some empowerment.

Lie down in a safe, comfortable place and take a few deep, centering breaths. Close your eyes and relax your body.

You find yourself in a vast open space, the sun shining bright in the sky. The day is warm and cloudless. In front of you, a figure is moving quickly toward you. The goddess Durga comes into view, riding her fierce golden tiger, holding aloft her hands, which are filled with weapons. She stops in front of you and stares at you with dark eyes.

"Greetings, child. I am Durga Maa, protectress and warrior mother. You have come to me when your path is uncertain, when the road ahead is plagued with obstacles. You have the power to overcome anything; know that. There is untapped courage that flows within you, and we shall access it now."

She motions for you to climb behind her on the tiger. Follow her lead and get on the great golden tiger.

"When you ride Durga's Tiger, there is nothing that you can't do."

She laughs, and the tiger moves quickly, launching forward across the plains. As you move, notice how free, empowered, and confident you feel. The wind is on your skin and the strength of the goddess surrounds you.

"You can overcome and rise above all fears, my child. Durga and her tiger of strength can help you to leap any canyon."

As she says this, you come to a great ravine, and in one leap, the tiger bounds over the chasm. You have no fear, no worries about it not working out. You know everything will work out. The goddess and her tiger stop on the other side of the ravine, and she helps you to the ground.

"Find me and my great tiger when you need to connect with empowerment. And never forget the courage that flows within you."

Bring your attention back to your body, slowly open your eyes, and take a few deep breaths. As you step back into your day, take Durga's guidance and messages with you.

DURGA · WARRIOR GODDESS OF STRENGTH

Matters Associated with Durga

* Truth
* Stepping into our power
* Taking action
* Awakening
* Finding our strength and fierceness
* Embracing leadership
* Getting help when we're in trouble or in need
* Slaying issues or problems
* Empowerment
* Death and destruction

Durga Affirmation

"I honor my truth. I embody strength and courage. I move confidently forward on my path. I will not back down. I am fierce. I am protected. I am strong."

Durga Associations

CRYSTALS	Carnelian, citrine, garnet, ruby, red agate, orange calcite
COLORS	Red, yellow
PLANTS & OILS	Sacred fig, banyan, sacred lotus, butterfly pea, hibiscus, arjun tree, correa, mango, coconut
ARCHETYPES	Warrior Goddess. Protective Mother. Goddess of Strength.
SYMBOLS	Tiger, buffalo, lion, swords, weapons.

EXPRESSING ANGER

Society teaches us we need to bottle up our anger, appear pleasant, and keep fierce emotions hidden. This can cause stress, sickness, and even death. Sometimes it can be hard for us to express our powerful feelings, but the goddess Durga can help. Here are ways that we can connect with and express our anger.

Yell it out. Go to a place where you will not be disturbed. This can be outside, somewhere you are alone in your home, or anywhere that you feel comfortable. Now, yell. Express the anger that is bubbling. Often, we need an outlet for our rage. Voicing it in a way that we are usually told we need to silence can help us to begin to process what is behind the anger. You can also envision telling the person with whom you are angry how you feel. This can help you connect with where your anger lies and aid in expression.

Take the pressure off. Do an activity that gets you into your body. This isn't to silence your anger, but it helps move the excess energy so you can tap into the anger's root cause. Dancing, singing, exercise, yoga, or walking, for example, can help.

Put it into words. Once you have taken the pressure off, it's time to tap into the root cause of your anger and put it into words. If you have a hard time finding the words, write it out first. Take some time to journal your anger.

Speak it. If you are angry with someone, you need to tell them why. Once you have connected to the root of what is upsetting you, you can more easily speak your truth. Formulate what you want to tell them and be honest with how you are feeling.

You can also receive help from the goddess Durga by lighting a red candle and saying:

"Goddess Durga, lady of rage,
Help me now to turn the page.
Let me express the anger I feel;
Allow my truth, so I express what's real.
Durga Maa, help my words to flow
So I can express, so I can let go."

STANDING OUR GROUND

Durga and her fierce tiger can help us stand our ground and stand up for ourselves when the world tries to push us around.

Find a solid, flat place in your home or outdoors. Stand with your feet shoulder-width apart and root your feet firmly into the earth. Envision roots coming out of your feet, anchoring you in place solidly.

Raise your hands up to the sky, allowing your fingers to touch in the middle. Stand strong and tall. In yoga this is called Mountain Pose, or **Tadasana**. Feel yourself strong, firm, and solid against the world. There is nothing you cannot face and nothing you cannot do.

Draw up strength from the earth and know that nothing can move you unless you wish to be moved. When you are finished, bring your arms back to your sides and shake out your body.

SHIELD OF POWER

The goddess Durga has ridden her fierce tiger into battle brandishing swords, knives, and lances from her many hands. She also holds a shield to protect herself and her followers from harm. In this practice, we use the shield of Durga to block the intentions of others and take back our power.

SUPPLIES
Candle
Something reflective that is easy to hold away from you,
    such as a compact mirror,
    a piece of metal,
    a piece of glass, or the lid of a pot
Something to squish, such as a grape on a plate

Carve the name of the person or organization that you need shielding from onto the candle. Light the candle. Hold the reflective item in your hands, point it toward the candle, and say:

> *"Shield of Durga, protect me now.*
> *Lend me your power as I will not bow.*
> *I will not break for those who wish*
> *And those who try, their wills I squish.*
> *With my shield held high, I will not fall.*
> *Durga Maa, your power I call.*
> *Reflect their evil back for them to see.*
> *As I will it, so shall it be."*

Squish the grape and envision the will of your enemy toward you thwarted. Discard the item away from you. Keep your shield near you, pointed outwards toward harm.

LEADERSHIP RITUAL

Durga connects us with our truth and our empowerment. She asks us to step into our power and lead from this place. With this ritual, we can connect deeper with our leadership role when we are called to take charge.

SUPPLIES
Red candle

Light the candle. Envision the leadership role you are stepping into or the one you want to take on and say:

> *"I am here to bring my truth into this world. On this path, I am here to embody a leadership role. I vow to honor this role and never to take it for granted or use it to lessen others. I honor my ability to bring my medicine into the world and lead from a place of humility, courage, and strength. I trust in my medicine and my intuition to lead me on this path. Guide me, Durga Maa, so that I may lead from a place of my deepest truth."*

19

CIRCE

THE SORCERESS

THE SORCERESS

THE WITCH

THE PRIESTESS

Circe (or Kirke) is the Greek goddess of sorcery, magick, rituals, and spellcraft. She is the daughter of the sun god Helios and the Oceanid nymph Perse. Sometimes she is said to be the daughter of Hecate, goddess of magick. In most of her myths, she was banished to the island of Aeaea by her father, left to craft her spells and rituals in solitude as punishment for her disobedience.

CIRCE INVOCATION

"Circe, lend me your magick so that I can protect myself against those who would do me harm. Grant me your power so that I, too, can offer retribution to those who would push their will upon me. Gift me your strength, so that I can stand alone in my power and cultivate my deeper truth. Let me acknowledge the sorceress that flows in my veins and embrace the medicine of all that I am."

CIRCE was a passionate and wild feminine force who has pursued lovers voraciously with her seductive advances. When jilted, she would often angrily change their forms into animals. She loved to transform humans, especially men, into beasts. She is said to carry a magical wand or staff that enhances her sorcery. Circe is a powerful feminine aspect of freedom, sacred magick, and passion. She lives freely, crafting her spells and potions as she sees fit. She was not destroyed by her banishment; it made her stronger. She is known for her transformation and illusion spells and her knowledge of the magic in every herb.

Circe swiftly sought retribution for the harm that others would visit upon her. When men tried to push their will on her, she transformed them into beasts with her powerful sorcery. In the myth of Odysseus, king of Ithaca, she turned his companions into pigs for trespassing on her island and only he was spared. In the book *Circe* by Madeline Miller, she transformed them because they found out she lived alone and intended to rape her. Odysseus petitioned her to turn them back in exchange for his staying with her for a time. Together they had three children over the years.

Though her punishments are often thought harsh, Circe teaches us to stand up for our rights, using our power to protect ourselves. We are not here to be trespassed by the will of others. We need to stand our ground and say no.

WALKING THE SOLITARY PATH

In most myths, Circe was banished to live a life alone on the island of Aeaea as punishment for her actions. This retribution was an attempt to silence her power, but her power grew in her solitude. On her sacred island, she cultivated a deep knowledge of magick, plants, and spells. There may be times when we walk a solitary path, but we too can come out of it more powerful than ever and reclaim our own magick.

Lie down in a safe, comfortable place and take a few deep, centering breaths. Close your eyes and relax your body.

You find yourself on a tall, vast cliff overlooking the ocean. There is nothing on the horizon in front of you; it melts into the sky. Turn around and find yourself on a lush island with a small hut in the distance. As you walk toward the small cabin, a woman with wild hair and eyes dark as the seas emerges.

"Welcome to the island of Aeaea. I am the sorceress Circe. They were afraid of my magick, and they banished me to this place, hoping to kill my spirit with solitude and dull my magick with their wrath. But they failed spectacularly. You cannot diminish the power of the sorceress with loneliness; it merely sharpens her blade and hones her skills. At times, each of us must walk the path of our practice in solitude. When we learn to tap into our inner knowing and embody the power of the sorceress, there is nothing and nowhere that they can place us where we will not thrive. Come, stand with me and root yourself deep in your own power!"

Stand with Circe and follow her as she raises her hands to the sky.

"I acknowledge my divine power as sorceress, the lineage of ancient knowledge that flows within my veins. Loneliness does not diminish me; it deepens my strength and wisdom. I am resilient. I am strong. I am filled with courage."

Say the words with her and feel a surge of power filling you. Feel yourself connecting deeper to ancient knowledge and the secrets of the Earth.

"Come here anytime you feel the need to tap into your strength. I will always be here, crafting my magic and growing in strength. Never forget the power that flows in your veins, for it is within you always."

Bring your attention back to your body, slowly open your eyes, and take a few deep breaths. As you step back into your day, take Circe's guidance and messages with you.

CIRCE · THE SORCERESS

Matters Associated with Circe

* Transformation
* Taking on a new form
* Working alone
* Connection with one's true purpose
* Spellcraft and rituals
* Standing up to the will of others
* Standing up against oppression
* Protecting ourselves using spellcraft
* Setting boundaries
* Thriving in solitude
* Vengeance

Circe Affirmation

"I protect myself from those who wish me ill. I guard against those who would trespass my boundaries. I stand up to those who would bend my will to fit theirs. I tap into the magick that flows within my veins. I am powerful. I cultivate great wisdom in my times of solitude."

Circe Associations

CRYSTALS	Tourmalinated quartz, black tourmaline, smoky quartz, labradorite
COLORS	Black, white, gray
PLANTS & OILS	Belladonna (poisonous), bergamot, mandrake (poisonous), bay, myrrh, vervain, wormwood (toxic)
ARCHETYPES	The Sorceress. The Witch. The Priestess.
SYMBOLS	Crescent moon, staff, wand

CREATING SACRED SPACE

Circe had a whole island dedicated as her sacred space on which to create spells and rituals. We can create a sacred space for ourselves anywhere we want a focal point for our rituals and spells and a touchstone for intentions and manifestation.

SUPPLIES

An area for your sacred space that will not be disturbed.
    Choose somewhere safe from children and pets, as they can get curious about candles or herbs. This can be a table, a spot on a dresser, or a whole room dedicated to your workings.
Sage, moon water, crystals, statues, or items that call to you
Bowls and bottles of herbs

To clear your sacred space, light some sage and sweep it through the air, envisioning the impurities dissipating. If you can't use smoke, use an infusion of moon water placed in a spray bottle with a few clearing crystals, such as citrine or rutilated quartz. Or, pass a piece of selenite or quartz and through the air. Place selenite around the room, for example a small piece tucked above the door trim, for continued cleansing. Optionally, say:

"I cleanse this space, I clear this room,
Within these walls, my powers bloom."

Make a dedication to your sacred space to charge it for what you want to accomplish. For example:

"This sacred space, I dedicate
To all the magick I will create.
May this space be shielded from all harm
Even after I work my spell or charm.
Sorceress Circe, watch over this space, this rite, and me.
As I will it, so shall it be."

POPPET SPELL

Poppets are humanesque forms created as an effigy of a person for the intent of spellcraft. Use these forms in either protective or banishing rituals; the poppet is imbued with something personal from the individual intended or, in self-directed blessings or manifestations, crafted in one's own image.

POPPET TO REPEL OR BANISH

SUPPLIES
Black candle
Pliable dried grasses or reeds
String
A tag or item belonging to the intended person
Fire
Banishing and protection herbs: rosemary, cumin, bay, or burdock

Light the candle. Shape a person out of the dried grass. It doesn't have to be perfect. Gather the bundle and tie off a section for the head. Tie another bundle together to form the arms and attach them to the main body. Affix the tag to the poppet. Say:

"Goddess Circe, lady of sorcery,
I petition to banish the attentions of (name) from me;
Block their aim, let them forget my name.
On the punishment of the Goddesses pain,
Have them leave me be. I am now free.
Never again will they bother me.
So it is."

Burn the item in a fire and offer the herbs to the flame as well.

POPPET TO DRAW OR MANIFEST

SUPPLIES
White candle
Cotton or linen cloth
Fabric pen or pencil
Scissors
Thread and needle
Batting
Manifestation and drawing herbs: balm of Gilead, ginger, sage, or cinnamon
Rutilated quartz and citrine
A tag or something of yours
Ribbon

Light the candle. Trace a gingerbread person shape onto the cloth, cut it out, and stitch it together. Stuff the poppet with batting, herbs, and crystals, and affix your tag. You can also write down what you wish to draw to you on a ribbon and tie it to the poppet. Say:

"Goddess Circe, hear my plea,
Direct good things toward me.
As I create this effigy,
What I desire comes to me."

Keep the poppet somewhere safe where you can cast it positive intentions and add more ribbons of desire when needed. For example, you could keep it on your altar or somewhere you will see it often, such as in your bedroom.

PROTECTION SALT

Protection salt is an easy-to-create substance you can use in rituals, protection rites, spells, and whenever you need protection. You can craft it during the full moon and leave it to charge in the moonlight.

SUPPLIES
Anise, Bay leaf, Fennel, Rosemary, Sage
Mortar and pestle (or blender)
Bowl
Sea salt
Airtight jar or container
Black candle
Pin

Grind the herbs until fine in a mortar and pestle or blender. If you don't feel called to grind them, crush them into smaller pieces. Transfer them to a bowl. Add salt and combine. Light the candle and say:

"Circe, goddess of sorcery,
I call now your protective energy to me.
This salt I create will block those with hate
And reflect back bad intentions sent toward me.
As you punished those who wronged you,
So shall I, too."

Place protective salt in the jar to store until needed. If you feel called to, drip some candlewax on the top of the jar lid. When it has cooled slightly, carve a protective symbol, such as an eye, two crossed spears, or the protection rune Algiz ᛉ, in it. (Algiz is a Y-shaped trident or upside down peace sign.)

SHATTERING ILLUSIONS

Circe is a powerful sorceress with the ability to change anyone into any form she desires, controlling and manipulating illusion as she saw fit. In this ritual, we will let our illusions take the form of ice and shatter that which has frozen us or blocked our pathway.

SUPPLIES

Water
Small freezer-safe container
Pin or carving tool

Pour the water into the container and freeze it. When it is solid, carefully etch what you wish to shatter upon it. This can be any illusion you hold, such as the illusion of your powerlessness or an illusion you hold in a relationship. When you have finished etching, say:

"Goddess of illusion, these illusions I break.
Dissolve the disillusion, the shroud from my eyes take.
Now all I see, is clarity;
Take these blockages away from me."

Break the ice on the ground and allow it to melt away. Envision the illusion shattering and melting away.

20

YEMAYA

GODDESS OF THE SACRED WATERS

- - - ● ● ● - - -

QUEEN OF THE SEA

MOTHER OF ALL

GUARDIAN OF WOMEN

PROTECTRESS

LADY OF THE MOON

- - - ● ● ● - - -

The goddess Yemaya is the Yoruban Queen of the Sea. She is considered the Mother of All and a protectress of women and children. Connected to the energy of the moon, she is the keeper of the divine feminine mysteries and cycles of the womb.

YEMAYA INVOCATION

"Oh lady of the sacred waters, to you and through you all life flows. You, who cradle all within a mother's arms. You, who hold the sacred feminine mysteries within your dark womb. I surrender all that no longer serves me to your seas and embrace your blessings. I release all that weighs me down to your waters. Within your sacred seas, I am reborn, cleansed of all I no longer need."

THOUGH her roots are in Africa, Yemaya was brought to the colonial world by enslaved Africans; she is celebrated in Cuba, Brazil, Haiti, and the United States. She was a very important orisha (deity) in Cuban Santeria, but its practices were outlawed under colonial Spanish rule. Yemaya was merged with the Virgin Mary by her followers so she could be celebrated more openly under the oppressive yoke of Catholic rule.

Yemaya is the daughter of the creative force of the universe, Olodumare. She is worshiped as an embodiment of the elemental force of water and the power wrought by the sea. She is sometimes depicted as a mermaid or with pearls beaded in the gleaming dark waves of her hair.

As a force of nature, Yemaya can be nourishing and life-giving, providing food and protection for her children. But she had a dark side, sending storms and chaos to those who offer her or her followers threat or ill will. She is sometimes depicted as holding a blade and is said to bathe in the blood of those she strikes down.

Considered the Great Mother, Yemaya has a compassionate energy. She cleanses her children of sadness and negative energy, healing them with her vast reach and fathomless depths. She guards over expectant mothers and sits with them when they bring their children into the world.

Yemaya tells us there is great wisdom to be found in the depths of ourselves. Much like the endless leagues that lie beneath the waves, we contain unseen treasure and mystery. She beckons us into the deep, asking that we leave behind shallow living and embrace all that we are.

Yemaya reminds us there will be storms in life, and they will upset the once-still waters around us. But this too is vital, as it clears away the debris that sometimes collects when the surface becomes stagnant. As a healing goddess, Yemaya opens herself to our offerings, asking us to surrender what is no longer in alignment with our deepest truth. Her waters give us the ability to release and to feel deeply into what weighs upon us. All life comes from her deep and nourishing waters, and she has the power to absorb all ill. In her connection to the moon and the tides, she whispers that our lives are ever changing. All things are in a constant flow of rebirth and transformation. Yemaya asks that we give ourselves over to these changes and move with the cycles.

VISUALIZATION

SURRENDER TO THE SEA

At times in our lives, there can be so much weighing on us that it becomes too much to bear. The goddess Yemaya can be a powerful force for helping us let go of what burdens us.

Lie down in a safe, comfortable place and take a few deep, centering breaths. Close your eyes and relax your body.

You are standing on a beautiful beach, the ocean waves lapping gently at your feet. The water stretches out toward the horizon, blending sea and sky into a vibrant tapestry of blue. The sun is shining, and the birds are singing. Feel the calm energy flowing through you.

A figure among the waves beckons to you. Move into the sea toward her. The ocean feels wonderful against your skin and you can move effortlessly through the waves. You find yourself in the company of the goddess Yemaya, her bright eyes sparkling, pearls shining in her midnight hair, and beads of water sparkling like jewels upon her dark skin.

"My child, you have come here with the weight of the world upon your shoulders. Your burdens are heavy, but the Mother of All Waters can help you release what drags you down."

She motions to the sea.

"Here in these divine waters, all is healed; all is taken away. All that no longer serves and all that drains you is taken away."

Yemaya opens her arms wider and wider, and she seems to blend into the horizon, her arms becoming the horizon.

"Lay down your troubles into my water."

Lie back into the water and float effortlessly on the surface of the sea. You feel weightless, and you can feel stress flow from your body.

Matters Associated with Yemaya

* Connecting with the feminine mysteries and cycles
* Healing
* Water magic
* Conception, birth, and fertility
* Moon or sea dedication
* Surrender and release
* Clearing away negativity
* Blessings for travel on the sea
* Go deep: Don't stay in the shallows
* Pregnancy

Yemaya Affirmation

"I open to the depths of my divine wisdom. I release what no longer serves my highest purpose. I surrender to my deepet truth. I embrace the depths of my feelings and intuition. I honor my cycles and the cycles of nature. I embrace the mother and honor her wisdom."

Yemaya Associations

CRYSTALS	Pearl, moonstone, abalone, aqua aura, aquamarine, beach stones, coral, larimar, blue onyx, sea glass
COLORS	Blue, teal, silver, white
PLANTS & OILS	Water lily, moonflower, lotus, reeds
ARCHETYPES	Queen of the Sea. Mother of All. Guardian of Women. Protectress. Lady of the Moon.
SYMBOLS	Shell, mermaid, waves, fish, driftwood, crescent moon, salt, conch shell, white flowers, doves

"Surrender. Let go. Release all that is weighing you down. I now take away all that weighs heavily upon you. In my sacred waters, you are healed anew. If you have anything specific you wish to be taken from you, speak it to me."

Take a few minutes and tell Yemaya what you wish to surrender to her waters.

"All that was heavy is now lighter. All that was dark is now brighter. Come to me anytime you wish to be cleansed and reborn."

Walk back toward the shore, feeling light and at peace after your connection with Yemaya.

Bring your attention back to your body, slowly open your eyes, and take a few deep breaths. As you step back into your day, take Yemaya's guidance and messages with you.

CLEANSING SHOWER RITUAL

All water is sacred to the goddess Yemaya, so we can connect with her cleansing energy daily with a cleansing shower ritual. Do this each day or as a clearing practice before doing other rituals or practices.

SUPPLIES
Shower
Vessel with which to hold water, such as a pitcher (optional)

When you are under the flowing water of the shower, close your eyes if it is safe to do so, ensuring that you have proper footing. Feel the water flowing down your head, your back, and your body. Envision the sacred waters of Yemaya pouring over and through you, clearing away anything cluttering your energy. Picture the water clearing away blocked energy from your chakra points and from your body, leaving shimmering light in its place. Envision the waters taking everything that is no longer wanted down to the ground and pouring it away. If you do not have a shower, this can be done in the bath with a vessel to pour the water over your head.

As the water flows over you, say:

"All my pain, all my grief,
Yemaya, now, bring relief.
Cleanse my body, mind, heart, and soul.
Take all ill; leave me whole."

BEACH STONE RELEASE

The sacred waters of Yemaya are the perfect place for us to release what we wish to be rid of. In her vast waters, we can let go, find peace, and be cleansed.

SUPPLIES
Beach stone
Natural ink, such as charcoal from a fire or another rock with which to etch (optional)

Go to the beach and find a stone that calls to you. Hold it in your hand and pour into the stone the intention of what you wish to be rid of in your life. It can be a belief, a problem, or a bad habit, for example—anything weighing you down. Focus on it for a few minutes. If you feel called to, write a keyword on the stone in natural ink.

When you have infused the stone with your intention, say:

> *"Yemaya, Yemaya, to you I release.*
> *I let go of my problems and I find peace."*

Throw the stone into the water as far as you can, envisioning the issue going with it, leaving you feelings lighter. Focus on the feeling of letting go and leaving behind what you want to release. Offer thanks to the goddess Yemaya with a natural offering.

SHORE NO MORE: SAND RELEASE

Another way to tap into Yemaya's powers of release is a simple beachside ritual. Do this when waves lap the shore. You will need to find a clear beach surface you can write on.

SUPPLIES
Sandy beach
Stick
Natural offering

Find a stick and go down to the beach. Stand at the water's edge and form a picture in your mind of what you want to release from your life. It can be anything from a habit to negative thoughts. Use the stick to write on the sand what you want to release to Yemaya and say:

> *"Goddess Yemaya, lady of the sea,*
> *Take away all that no longer serves me.*

From what I wish to release, let me be free.
I am now unburdened; so shall it be."

Watch as Yemaya's waters come up to the shore and consume what you wish to release. With each wave dissolving the words, envision your issue flowing into the sea, into the arms of Yemaya, to be cleansed and taken away from your life. Thank the goddess and leave her a natural offering.

FERTILITY INVOCATION

Yemaya is connected to pregnant mothers and fertility. As a protectress of women and children, she can be a wonderful goddess for expectant mothers or those who wish to connect with her fertile, life-giving energy. Use this invocation to entreat Yemaya for her protection or aid if you are expecting a child or wish to conceive.

"I am relaxed and open in body, mind, heart, and spirit
To create the miracle of life.
I openly invite the abundance of fertility into my body and heart.
My womb is a fertile place of nourishment and love.
My reproductive organs are balanced, healthy, and harmonious.
They allow my body to conceive easily,
Supporting the miracle of life.
I open to the gift of life within me.
I am grateful to walk this path of creating life.
I am thankful for the blessings that I have.
I am excited and honored to wear the mantle of motherhood.
Divine creative energy flows through my body.
Miracles flow to me in every breath.
My home is a sanctuary of sacred energy
Supporting the conception of my child.
I embrace the love that I am creating and expanding.
I am at peace, in body, mind, heart, and spirit,
Knowing that the miracle of life flows easily to me.
Bless me, Mother Yemaya,
As your sacred waters run through me
And through all life."

Glossary

AFFIRMATION A statement or declaration asserting a specific empowering intention

ALTAR A sacred space dedicated to spiritual workings, offerings, and rites

ARCHETYPE A recurring type or symbol from myth or history associated with specific attributes

ASSOCIATIONS Attributes of a being or item that are connected to aspects such as planetary, plants, gemstones, or animals

AVALON An ancient island connected to Morgan La Fey, legends of King Arthur and Camelot

BANISHING Rejecting or casting something out of one's life intentionally

BINDING Prohibiting someone from causing harm using restrictive intentions and methods

BLESSING Words or deeds offered in reverence or thanks

CHARGING To infuse something with energy or intention

CLEARING To remove ill energy from a person or place

DARK NIGHT OF THE SOUL A period when we are faced with darkness, disconnection, fears, wounds, or uncertainty in our lives that leads to transformation, growth, and evolution

FAMILIAR Usually used in connection with an animal indicating a tie of a spiritual nature to whose medicine, meaning, or presence resonates with us

GODDESS A powerful female figure from myth or legend

GROUNDING Connecting to the Earth to create stability, release energy, and gain energy from the Earth

HEX An intentional ritual designed to repel, curse, or protect to be done when provoked or threatened

INCANTATION A spell that is verbal or said aloud

INTENTION A clarification of our purpose in order to set our desires or goals

INVOCATION To draw power to oneself or embody it

KARMA The belief that the nature of past actions dictates future luck or fate

MAGICK A thread of divine wisdom that breathes through the soul

MAIDEN, MOTHER, CRONE The triple aspect of the Goddess representing birth, life, and death

MANIFESTATION Making something tangible or real

OFFERING Herbs or other natural items given in thanks

OFFERING TO THE FIRE/RELEASING TO THE FIRE Letting go of what no longer serves us to the fire

OLD WAYS/OLD RELIGION An old system of beliefs tied toward earth medicine, natural healing, or possibly working with deities

PATRIARCHY An oppressive system that has been ruling for thousands of years that excludes and often blocks women, BIPOC, and LGBTQZIA+ people from equality, rights, opportunity, and power

POPPET A doll or totem used to draw energy to a specific person

PRIESTESS Someone who connects with the ancient rites and mysteries of the old ways; can be initiated into a specific path or work as a solitary priestess

RITUAL A ceremony of incantations, actions, or items that are meant to manifest intent

SANTERIA A religion with African roots that began in Cuba and spread through Latin America and the United States

SHIELDING A rite of protection

SMUDGE To burn dried herbs or plants to create sacred smoke to clear an area of stagnant or negative energy

SORCERESS Someone who practices the ancient rites and mysteries

STREGHERIA An Old Religion from Italy from hundreds of years ago

TEMPLE Sacred site of worship usually dedicated to a specific deity

TRIPLE GODDESS maiden, mother, crone

UNDERWORLD A mythological place where the souls of the dead go

VISUALIZATION A visual process to empower through mental imagery

WITCH Someone connected with the medicine and magick of the natural world, the mystery of the moon and open to the lessons of the unseen world. Can be dedicated to a specific tradition or a solitary practitioner.

Resources

A-Museing Grace Gallery—The Magical Art of Thalia Took. thaliatook.com

Auset, Brandi. *The Goddess Guide: Exploring the Attributes and Correspondences of the Divine Feminine.* Woodbury, MN: Llewellyn Publications, 2009.

"Baltic Mythology: Hunting Goddesses." Baltic Mythology and Paganism. balticmythology.tumblr.com/post/123969785359/baltic-mythology-hunting-goddesses

"Bastet." Gods & Goddesses. gods-and-goddesses.com/egyptian/bastet

Coco. "In the Very First Days: Inanna and Lilith." The Daily Revolution. dailyrevolution.org/thursday/inanna.html

"Conoce las semejanzas entre la Virgen de Guadalupe y la diosa Coatlicue." Parabólica: Perodismo en Red. parabolica.mx/2019/nacional/item/31478-conoce-las -semejanzas-entre-la-virgen-de-guadalupe-y-la-diosa-coatlicue

Cotterell, Arthur. *The Encyclopedia of Mythology.* Cambridgeshire, UK: Lorenz Books, 2016.

Cunningham, Scott. *Cunningham's Encyclopedia of Magical Herbs.* Woodbury, MN: Llewellyn Publications, 1985.

Dunwich, Gerina. *Wicca Candle Magick.* New York: Kensington Publishing Corporation, 2018.

"The Earth Gods." *Aztec History and Culture.* history-aztec.com/earth-gods.html

Eason, Cassandra. *The Complete Crystal Handbook: Your Guide to More Than 500 Crystals.* New York: Sterling, 2010.

"Egyptian Gods: Bastet." Egyptian Gods and Goddesses. egyptian-gods.org/egyptian-gods-bastet

"Egyptian Gods: Sekhmet." Egyptian Gods & Goddesses. egyptian-gods.org/egyptian-gods-sekhmet

"The Eye of Ra, a Powerful Symbol of Ancient Egypt with a Profound Meaning." Cleopatra Egypt Tours. cleopatraegypttours.com/travel-guide/the-eye-of-ra

George, Demetra and Douglas Bloch. *Asteroid Goddesses: The Mythology, Psychology, and Astrology of the Re-Emerging Feminine.* Lake Worth, FL: Ibis Press, 2003.

"Goddesses, Iguanas and More at Temple Ixchel," The Travel Current. thetravelcurrent.com/mexico/isla-mujeres/explore/culture/goddesses-iguanas -and-more-temple-ixchel-isla-mujeres

Grimassi, Raven. *The Book of the Holy Strega.* Springfield, MA: Old Ways Press, 2012.

Grimassi, Raven. *Italian Witchcraft: The Old Religion of Southern Europe.* Woodbury, MN: Llewellyn Publications, 2003.

Hall, Judy. *The Crystal Bible.* New York: Penguin, 2003.

Heath, Maya. *Magical Oils by Moonlight*. Franklin Lakes, NJ: The Career Press, 2004.

Heathwitch. "Oya: Lady of Storms." The White Moon Order.
orderwhitemoon.org/goddess/oya-storms/Oya.html

"Inanna." Let ME Go. creative-catalyst.com/letmego/inanna.html

Ille, Judika. *Encyclopedia of Spirits: The Ultimate Guide to the Magic of Fairies, Genies, Demons, Ghosts, Gods, and Goddesses*. New York: HarperOne, 2009.

Kempton, Sally. *Awakening Shakti: The Transformative Power of the Goddesses of Yoga*. Boulder, CO: Sounds True, 2013.

Kharal, Syma. *Goddess Reclaimed: 13 Initiations to Unleash Your Sacred Feminine Power*. Toronto: Flourishing Goddess, 2017.

Kynes, Sandra. *Llewellyn's Complete Book of Correspondences: A Comprehensive & Cross-Referenced Resource for Pagans & Wiccans*. Woodbury, MN: Llewellyn Publications, 2013.

Lewis, Dave. "Priestess Reveals Secrets of Glastonbury's Goddess Temple." Somerset Live.
somersetlive.co.uk/news/local-news/priestess-reveals-secrets-glastonburys
-goddess-3329789

Mahalik, Gyanranjan and Sagarika Parida. "Study on the Use of Plants and Plant Parts in Durga Puja for Worshipping of the Goddess Durga in Odisha, India. *International Journal of Technology Management* 8 (11): 2911–2918.

"Moon Offerings: Oils and Waters." jesterbear.com/Aradia/MoonOfferings.html

Smith, William and Chris Stray. A *Dictionary of Greek and Roman Biography and Mythology*. CC Little and J. Brown, 1849.

Snider, Amber C. "The History of Yemaya, Santeria's Queenly Ocean Goddess Mermaid." *Teen Vogue*. teenvogue.com/story/the-history-of-yemaya-goddess-mermaid

Telyndru, Jhenah. "The Goddesses of Avalon." Jhenah Telynoru: Walking the Priestess Path. ynysafallon.com/writings/the-goddesses-of-avalon

Webley, Kayla. "Coatlicue." *Time*. content.time.com/time/specials/packages/article /0,28804,2066721_2066724_2066733,00.html

Wolkstein, Diane and Samuel Noah Kramer. "Gilgamesh Epic, Tablet 12." jewishchristianlit.com/Texts/ANEmyths/gilgamesh12.html

Wright, Gregory. "Morrigan." Mythopedia. mythopedia.com/celtic-mythology/gods/morrigan

Young Yamanaka, Katie. "Pele, Goddess of Fire and Volcanoes." Hawaii.com. www.hawaii .com/discover/culture/pele

About the Author

C. ARA CAMPBELL is a visionary writer, author, and founder of The Goddess Circle. She is a soul guide, cosmic channel, facilitator of the *Inner Priestess Awakening Journey* and the *Relationship Empowerment and Sacred Love Journey,* and author of *The Astro Forecast Publication.* She is a contributing author to the books *Journeys with the Divine Feminine* and *Original Resistance: Reclaiming Lilith, Reclaiming Ourselves.* Ara is a modern-day mystic dedicated to empowering others and connecting them with their purpose, living embodied truth, and healing using the natural world. She has a lifelong connection to the stories of the Goddess. Ara is an old soul who been writing and channeling guidance from the unseen since she was young, intuitively soul coaching using spiritual and natural energies and the insight of the stars. She can often be found seeking wisdom and solace in the wilds of Mother Earth, capturing the magic of nature with her camera, or snuggling her dog, Sonny.

Acknowledgments

To all those who have walked with me on this path and made this dream a reality, I thank you.

I would like to acknowledge all of the wonderful people at Fair Winds Press and Quarto Publishing for this amazing experience and for making this dream come true. I would like to thank all of the people that I have been honored to connect with on this journey over the years. I am so grateful for those I have come to know around the world in friendship and fellowship. Thank you for your connection through The Goddess Circle.

I would like to thank my family and friends for their support and love. Your encouragement is so appreciated. Special thanks to my mom, who has always been my number one fan, thank you for cheering me on from day one. My sister, for her dedication to my vision for The Goddess Circle; thank you for your talent and hilarious sense of humor. To my partner, thank you for standing by me and for always supporting me. It means more than you will ever know. And to my dog Sonny for his boundless enthusiasm, cuddles, and eternal love.

Index